Congratulations!
You Just
Lost Your Job

COMPILED BY
LaSean Rinique

Congratulations! You Just Lost Your Job
©2014 by LaSean Rinique

ISBN: 1500572675

Printed in the United States of America

con·grat·u·la·tions

kən͵graCHə'lāSHəns,-͵grajə-/

noun

1. An expression of praise for an achievement or good wishes on a special occasion; the act of congratulating.

Yes, losing your job can be traumatic, especially in these trying economic times, but it can also be your New Beginning to the rest of your life story. In CONGRATULATIONS! YOU JUST LOST YOUR J.O.B., the authors gladly and candidly share with you one of the most important journeys of their life: the voyage from employee to entrepreneur.

Many people claim they want to become an entrepreneur; however, after a few no's or when things don't progress as they hoped, they mistake the process of necessary growth and development as failure. Perseverance, dedication, resiliency, and trial and error are all important ingredients in the recipe for success. The authors whose words are penned herein include those who have tried every home-based business, failed miserably on a first attempt, and some who were ultimately heartbroken when their J.O.B. (just over broke, your sense of security) was pulled out from under them. This book will help you rethink the losing of your job, help you see it as the blessing it is!

Imagine working 40 hours a week for 40 years, only to receive 40% of your pay. If you struggled while earning that, what makes you think retirement will be any better?

Time is one of the most valuable resources you have, and you can never get it back. How many recitals, plays, games, first steps, loose teeth, and holidays have you missed while toiling away at your J.O.B.? Has time slipped away so fast that it seems like your child went from birth to college in one day? The good news is that there *is* still time for change.

Our employers want us to be healthy, well enough to work, yet we have to ask permission to go to a dental appointment or visit a doctor. Why should one have to choose between lost pay, burning up vacation days, or wellness? That just does not seem fair at all!

The people you'll read about here finally decided that these things and more mattered, and so do they! In their case—and quite possibly in yours—losing a J.O.B. actually changed lives for the better. What a gift!

This book is not for the happy, fulfilled employee who finds extreme joy and satisfaction in their work, especially if that work is their passion. Rather, these stories were compiled as a resource and encouragement for those who are clocking in for the pay rather than the purpose. If you find yourself digging for excuses to get out of going to that J.O.B., this book is for you, my friend!

This book is dedicated to hardworking entrepreneurs
who toiled away for too many long, hard hours,
only to help someone else achieve a dream,
only to suddenly find the courage to do it for themselves.

For Anthony-Marc, JiHaad-Harmeen, and Aliya-Bernice.
Mommy loves you!

ACKNOWLEDGMENTS

$\mathcal{S}$o many thank-you's and shout-outs go to all those who believed in us, but also to those who did not!

First of all, to God, my strength and my light!

Also, to my family – Bernice Elizabeth James, you are my angel who never leaves my side; although I cannot see you, I feel your presence every day. I love you, Mom! I love you, Mom! To my dad, Ronald James Sr.; my brothers (Ronald James Jr., Omar James, and Kevin Shelton); my sisters (Empress Henderson, Carrie Day, Cervantez Shelton, and Ella Shelton); my nieces and nephews (Justice, Noble, Greyson, Taylor, Marcus, Simone, Xavier, Solomon, Anna, Brely, Zach, Ericka, Naomi, Sarah, and Laura, Kam'Dyn, Kam'Ryn); my cousins (Tania Martin, Sean Wells, Starr Talley, Ronda Foxworth, Veronica Jackson, Belinda Ealey, and Ruth Underwood): the love of my life, Al Stevens; and my babies (Maximillian, Rajnesh, Dior, Shianna, and Alicia Stevens).

Special thanks also to Mother Rosario, Pastor Beaman, and the Beaman family and the Bethel AME Wilmington family. To my sister-girls (Pamela Lamb, Sheena Lowe, Arreda Cotton, Reverend Regina Gray, L'Tanya (I-Am D One) Taylor, Dionne Dimples Dendy, Nellie Davis, Montrell Ming Lee Ward, Tanny Collins, O'Neida Stevenson, Trina Jacobs, Dr. Selena Griffith, Angie Fitch, Shavaya Matthews, Alicia Hill, and many more). To Charles Edwards, Jessica "GaGa" Asan, Paulie, Lashawn Pryor, Tiana Von Johnson, and Carl Stokes. To Zeta Phi Beta Sorority and Phi Beta Sigma Fraternity, my extended family of the divine nine, Peak Performers Institute, Che and Trevor, Lamont Belton, the Cullen's Corner family, the DSU Chat.

Most of all, a heartfelt thank-you to all CONGRATULATIONS! YOU JUST LOST YOUR J.O.B. co-authors and their family.

If you feel you should have been on this list and I forgot your name, charge my mind, not my heart!

FOREWORD

by Kevin S. Wilson

*A*s an entrepreneur both at heart and in practice, it is very easy to relate to the stories in this book. Many of us struggle to find proper balance in our lives between family, work, and interests. The stories of the contributors in this book help us find balance, perspective, and relativity in our own very unique situations.

We all want to find ways to improve our lives. Oftentimes, we think this means more money. As you will discover in many of these stories, you must first pursue your passion to attain what is really most important, your own happiness.

As a personal finance expert, I can tell you that the relativity of money is tremendous. What is most important is that we have a happiness plan, and we must perform the necessary actions to meet our goals. Money should be a tool in our pursuit of happiness, not a master to enslave us in our pursuits for the sake of what we can buy with it and the so-called status it will bring.

We are all responsible for defining our own happiness. However, on a general level, it comes from doing what we enjoy in order to provide for the ones we love. These authors' stories resonate with the need to have an action plan. Enjoy and learn from these stories, and admire their motivating qualities that will help you in your own life.

To learn more about Kevin S. Wilson, please visit
www.womantalkbook.com

FOREWORD

Dr. Tiana Von Johnson

*E*very day, each of us are blessed with 86,400 seconds to fulfill a dream. Each second brings us closer to success, as long as those seconds are used wisely. Life is all about making wise choices and maximizing opportunities. Our mindset must demonstrate the desires of our hearts if we are to make the changes we want to see in the world. Life will not hand us success, focus, faith, and determination. All life hands us is an empty canvas, and it is up to you to paint the picture your heart desires. What will you paint?

As a mindset coach and serial entrepreneur, I have seen many dreams vanish simply because people thought them unattainable, too hard, or not within their reach. Worst of all, they did not feel they deserved success. Why does it seem so impossible to become a millionaire and/or your own successful boss? Any willing person can become that iconic hero, if you just put your mind to it.

By all accounts, my life has been a testimony. I started out as a street vendor, selling records in Harlem with my dad, and became one of the most powerful names in real estate. I did not wake up closing deals for celebrities or people of influence; rather, I had to change my mindset and envision myself becoming successful. I had to brand myself as a power house in my industry. Once I did, people began believing in me. Why? Because I BELIEVED IN ME! Within my first year in business, I generated over one million dollars.

When I heard LaSean Rinique speak, I was blown away. In my mind, all I could say was, Wow! She gets it. I remember her words so vividly: "Change your perception, believe in yourself, and find your why that is strong enough to make you cry." She spoke about congratulating yourself for leaving that J.O.B., the just over broke or juggling overdue bills situation. She spoke about the mental, physical, spiritual, and emotional benefits of quitting what she referred to as the 40/40/40 Club. It was as though I was speaking through her to the hundreds of men and women I speak to and train every year. She was speaking to those people who so desperately need a mindset makeover.

At twenty-seven years old, after achieving some success in the corporate arena that I commonly refer to as the #9to5Life, I left a cushy highrise office and stepped out on faith, leaving my lucrative, six-figure salary behind. I borrowed money to attend real estate school. I had determination and a will to win, and I recognized that success is not linear. That is why I am where I am today. I have taken a journey, and it still is not over! From Wall Street, to television, to magazines, to earning my doctorate and traveling the country sharing my secrets of success, I know what it takes to succeed, and I'm going after my dreams like the air that I breathe.

CONGRATULATIONS! YOU JUST LOST YOUR J.O.B. is your pathway to success. LaSean has compiled stories from stellar entrepreneurs who share their journeys and offers tips, suggestions, and ways to become your own boss. I encourage everyone to read this book, and do not keep it a secret!

Spread the word. Fulfil your goals. BE your OWN boss!

Dr. Tiana Von Johnson

For more about Dr. Von Johnson:

The Mindset Makeover: How to Enhance Your Self-Worth to Increase Your Net-Worth available now on Amazon.com and eBook for Kindle.

Follow on Instagram, Twitter, Facebook and YouTube @ TianaVonJohnson – See more at: http://tianavonjohnson.com

TABLE OF CONTENTS

CEO

PRESIDENT

VICE PRESIDENT

MIDDLE MANAGEMENT

HARD WORKING EMPLOYEES

No Thanks... Looks Like a Pyramid Scheme

QUIT THE 40/40/40 CLUB

What is the 40/40/40 Club? It is when one works long and hard for forty years, investing plenty of blood, sweat, and tears, bartering for vacations, missing family events, and literally get physically ill from burnout and working so much; many illnesses can be attributed to lack of rest, poor eating habits, and stress. This monotonous, painful cycle continues for forty long years. It is said that forty years on a job or in a particular career should earn one enough savings and 401(k) benefits to last a lifetime. Social Security is no longer promised to us, however, and it has now become a privilege for us to see what we invested in for those forty-plus years. After those hard-working four decades, retirees are often forced to seek employment at local retail stores or restaurants, depending on minimum wage and tips to help them get by. Why? Because there was no Plan B, and that 40 percent is clearly not enough to live on and definitely not enough to put anything back in savings. If 100 percent of your net earnings was not enough, what would make you think 40 percent, a small fraction, will be enough to provide for you during the remainder of your years? This is the 40/40/40 Club, working 40 hours a week for 40 years, only to be expected to be able to live on 40 percent, which is a nearly impossible task.

This is why congratulations are in order when you lose your J.O.B., that just-over-broke, juggling-overdue-bills situation. Enough is enough!

Of course there are some employees who passionately enjoy what they do and are comfortable with their pay. This message is for the person who is looking for daily innovative excuses to call off work without getting fired. I am talking to the person who's been laid off, terminated, or has simply had enough. These stories will compel you to take a second and maybe even a third look at that everyday routine you call a J.O.B.

I use a holistic approach with my clients, an effort to heal and speak to the *whole* person. There's an emotional, physical, and mental benefit to this underlying blessing of losing your J.O.B. Think about it: You were cheating yourself out of so many good things that life has to offer. We're told to work hard and play hard; however, if your health is poor, you cannot enjoy the play. For example, how many times have you had to ask for your supervisor's permission to go to the doctor, dentist, therapist, or even your child's medical appointments? Maybe you've had to give up your hard-earned vacation time because you ran out of sick days due to a few challenges in life. In a perfect world, you, your relatives, and your pet would all get sick at the same time, so you could much more conveniently schedule wellness visits and checkups on the same day, and everyone would be cured immediately, but life doesn't work that way. Many times, these things happen in threes, and you find yourself having to barter time in order to keep your pay from being docked or your job from being lost.

You've also had to beg for time off to attend events that are important to your spouse, your child, or a friend; it means the world to them when you can attend, but of course those memorable occasions fall on a work day, and you cannot take off. How many times have you disappointed your friends or loved ones and have had to settle for watching those once-in-a-lifetime occasions on video because you had a project or a paper to grade? Missing these special events dilutes the family bond and causes friction, especially with the parent or caregiver who has to carry that particular torch alone in your absence.

Does it feel as if you were just in the delivery room on Tuesday, yet those babies are all grown up and in college by Thursday? Time waits for no one, and many executive have told sad tales, recounting that all the money in the world could not buy back a moment of time lost from their son's or daughter's childhood. Having to ask permission to spend time with your kids can be a very difficult experience; you will likely feel torn between having a good work ethic and being an example to those who look up to you or choosing to strengthen the family dynamic by being an interactive part of your children's everyday lives. When you feel forced to choose your J.O.B. over your family that is time you can't get back.

When will it be your turn to come first? When do you take care of you? When does your family get to see you and spend quality time with you? The answer is simple: Quit the 40/40/40 Club and give yourself the opportunity to invest the same energy on your gifts and talents and monetize from them. One fringe benefit your employer will never give you is being able to spend time doing what you love doing, with those who matter the most to you.

So, congratulations! You just lost your J.O.B.!

THE JOURNEY

Dr. Paulette Clark

*T*his is such a wonderful time to tell my story about why and how I became an entrepreneur. Ever since I was young girl, it was what I had been exposed to. Growing up in the Midwest in mainly ethnic communities, I was always exposed to those who owned a store, a garage, a daycare, or something of the sort that supplemented a full-time income.

This was what people did to make ends meet, and it was very natural. I literally could not tell you of one adult I knew during my childhood who was not moonlighting or doing something for themselves to add to what they had for that rainy day or school clothes for the kids.

I was taught very young how to earn my own money. My foster parents owned both a trucking company and a daycare and taught my foster siblings and me how to get creative to earn money. One year, they left it up to us to buy our own school clothes, so the four of us sat down to figure out how much money we would need for clothes and shoes for the upcoming year. We decided upon several things: We would have a carnival in the back yard each weekend, with games and rides for the neighborhood kids, and we would sell popcorn, cheese curls, and Now and Laters in tiny bags for twenty-five cents, all summer long.

By the end of that first summer, after a lot of hard work and in spite of competition that grew along the street from other children who noticed our efforts, we earned a healthy $91.23! Our foster mother split the money between us, and she matched what we made that year. How excited we were to take our earnings in little sandwich bags to

JL Marcus, the discount store on North Avenue, to buy our two outfits and two pairs of shoes for the beginning of the year! It was so empowering, and it felt so good.

We grew up and moved on to college and careers of our own, but to this day, we remain entrepreneurs. I attribute that to our foster mother, who instilled in us the love of making our own money.

One thing in particular that I learned early on, I would keep with me for years to come: If you are not happy with what you do, you won't do it well. So, fresh into my sophomore year of college, I packed up and moved to Atlanta, Georgia to begin a singing career. I loved singing more than anything in the world. As a vocalist at twenty-one years of age, I was paid by the gig. I was contracted to work for one of the hottest groups during the early nineties and made great money doing what I loved. I traveled a lot and was able to send money home to take care of my one-year-old daughter, who was in the care of my family, all of them living quite comfortably. However, I was not paying attention. As life would have it—not luck but life, mind you—I had the wool pulled over my eyes right in front of me. Before I knew it, I found myself without work. I had been replaced just as the group was reaching its pinnacle, winning awards all over the world, and a spin-off group I'd created was taken, marketed, and sold right out from under me. Imagine what that did to a young woman's spirit when she was only doing what she loved!

It was a sad experience, but I learned a valuable lesson from it: Always handle your business like your life depends on it, because it does. I was young and trusting and believed my so-called friends were looking out for me. They were really only looking out for themselves, and I lost out in the end as a result. I could have avoided it had I been more careful and sought representation in the form of an attorney and an accountant.

Licking my wounds and moving on with my life was very difficult. As I watched the group of people I'd trusted win award after award for work I had collaborated on, I lost touch with reality and had to regroup. During that time, I resorted to what I knew, recalling those folks back on the block, who all knew how to do something to pay the bills. I went back to college with the money I had left from touring and performances, and I used my talents to make money, from singing to braid hair—all while studying at night. As a busy student and a single mother of two, I did whatever was necessary to pay the bills and keep a roof over my children's heads. I often think back to those days and remember when I had nothing else beyond my voice and my hands. I could sing at weddings, provide sample vocals for an upcoming album, teach acting classes at the talent agency that booked all the video models for the hottest hip-hop artists of that time, and I could braid hair. I literally did not know how to work for anyone else, because at that point, I never really had. I had to figure out how to make it work being my own employee and my own boss.

After graduating from college in the late nineties, I finally secured full-time employment as a senior systems engineer. The money was great, but I truly hated all the politics. I had wonderful benefits, but the day-to-day grind of answering to someone else didn't exactly resonate within me, and I didn't think I'd be able to stick with it. Ultimately, I was right. I didn't stick it out and decided to contract myself out to major corporations for more money and less of my time. I found ways to actually outsource work that I did not know how to do, until that fateful day of September 11, 2001; literally within several days, many contractors, myself included, lost our positions. As horrible as it was, the Towers were not the only things that collapsed that day; our incomes were slashed and our lifestyles demolished far quicker than the years it had taken to build them up.

I had to think quickly and decided, *Okay, if I go back to braiding hair, I would be competing with everyone.* Though I had been blessed enough to be trained by the best in the business, even to this day, I knew the competition was fierce, and I am not African. What I did know was how to keep quiet and ride the waves. I also knew technology and how to write very well.

So, I decided to build a firm that would work with artists seeking press and public relations for their upcoming projects or events. It would take some hard work and networking to bring my idea to fruition, though, as well as time I didn't have. I took on a couple clients, and Enterliant Group was born: "Enter" for "entertainment" and "liant" from "reliant." We were a group because I worked with a few trusted people to get things done. The name was such a perfect fit that I eventually incorporated myself and took on a part-time job working tables overnight to supplement my income.

Still, the economy was not picking up fast enough in Atlanta, so I had to make a decision. Before my children and I ended up on the streets, I needed to move to a more economically sound area. I decided to transfer to the home of my birth father, who owned some land and had been encouraging me, "Come home." I sold everything I owned, packed up my little family (now myself and three daughters) and moved to Arkansas.

Talk about a culture shock! No one in Arkansas cared who I was, nor did they want to know. There was no city life, nor were there many avenues for networking. I felt defeated and out of sorts. I sat still for literally two years, trying figure out what my next move should be. What I didn't know was that those two years would turn out to be a great time of growth and reflection for me to prepare me for the next opportunities that were coming my way. I did the only thing I knew how to do: Again, I resorted to braiding hair and singing at local functions for cash, and I even worked at a bomb-making plant for pennies. During that time, I decided one more round of college wouldn't hurt me either, so I headed back to school while I struggled to make sense of everything that had happened.

Once I had become acclimated to country living, I decided to open a consignment shop in south Arkansas, and it actually did very well. I tried to work for someone else, but it simply did not seem to be the best option for me; I never felt like I was in control while I was an employee. My consignment store and swap meet housed several offices in the rear, and over the years, I was often asked to work on local events and other campaigns throughout the state. By referral only, people began to come to me for things they needed help with. It started with a press release, then a commercial, then a press release *and* a commercial. Word got around that I could do much more, and influential people began to call on me for support in things that were happening statewide. From proposals to press releases, social media, web design, customer service, public relations, and more, I found myself doing more and more PR work than consignment work—so much so that I eventually closed the shop but kept the offices.

During this time, I began to host events, networking with local and state politicians, and really got my feet back in the game. I learned how to keep my head low and tell the story that needed to be told for my clients. I reached back into my history and used every skill and lesson I'd ever learned to grow my virtual database of clients; to this day, they still reach out to me when they need public and community relations, web design, social media support, marketing, or someone to help clean up a public mess.

Enterliant Services Group is a company built on many years of hard work and referrals. I certainly sound like a modern-day Olivia Pope, but we do exist. We are the silent people, the ones handling things behind the scenes that no one wants to believe are real, all while husbands go to work and wives are able to stay home with babies. I still pride myself on being able to manage major events. We hire customer support professionals who work directly with our clients on a day-to-day basis, yet we still keep our heads low and get the job done.

Do I still braid hair? Sometimes, but you have to catch me in good mood. I still do voice work, only now I am paid for my voiceover work for clients who need a complete package, as well as my public and community relations services. I am the busiest, of course, during political seasons here in the state, and yes, I do sometimes have to take a mop and broom and clean up some things I've been sworn never to discuss, but I love what I do.

Sometimes I look back and think about the journey I took to get here and the stories I have to tell about living life as a business owner. I can't say it's always been easy, but I most certainly would not have it any other way.

There are many lessons I have learned along the way, and I would love to share them with you:

Handle your own business. Write your own checks and everyone else's. No one ever needs to know what you are making before you do. There is way too much technology out there for you not to be able to do this with relative ease.

Never allow anyone to be *your* voice. If you allow someone to speak for you, you will always be misunderstood. Do not be elusive; quite frankly, you ain't that fabulous!

Know *daily* how much you are making. Never go to bed without know what you made that day. This means you have to wake up each day know what you are going to make, and you have to know what you have to do to make that happen. To this day, I keep a little notebook with me. In it, I write a list of six things to do, a tip I learned from Zig Ziglar. I also write down how much money I want to make and how much I actually do.

Pay your people first, and treat them like people. Understand that no one *has* to work for you. I have never thrown people away who've worked for me; instead, they've fired themselves over and again. If I find someone is weak in one area, I will certainly find another place for that person to be, where they can be more effective. My employees can choose to stay or go; ultimately, that decision is theirs.

Network. My network is different. People do not find out about me from business cards or a website but from word-of-mouth referrals. That said, I would encourage you to get business cards, build a website, and be social.

Put your money where your mouth is. Always invest in you. Take a class, go back to school, enhance what you know, or spend money on advertising and marketing if you need to. No one is going to invest or believe in you if you are not willing to do the same for yourself.

Make sure you can change with the times. This, too, shall pass. As I write this, Enterliant Services Group now offers call center opportunities. I am excited about this as we expand and grow and are able to help people earn a decent wage. No matter what, don't become stagnant. Adapt and change when you have to, and always be on the lookout for new things to enhance what you do and enjoy doing. Enterliant Group will always be the PR firm you've never heard about, and I'm okay with that. We will always do what we have always done, only now we can help others feed their families.

Find mutually beneficial friends and mentors. Birds of a feather flock together, a lesson I was taught early on in life. Thus, surround yourself with likeminded people who are doing *better* than you are. Connect with them and glean from them what you can, and make sure you give back when you can.

You ain't that bad. No matter what your loyal followers say or how many compliments and rave reviews you get, you are not that good. There is always someone out there who does it better than you, on less of a budget. There is always room for improvement in everything you do, so never stop learning about your craft, and never hesitate to pick up a new skill that will help your business grow.

Enjoy the ride! If you truly do what you love, if it is your passion, everything else will take care of itself. Make sure you don't mind waking up doing what you are doing. Make sure you feel as if you could do it for free, that when you are working your business, you are flying so high that time seems to get away from you. Embrace this time as an entrepreneur and the joys and challenges that go along with it. me with it. Of course it's not easy, but it's so very, very worth it!

I hope you have been able to find a lesson in my story, for I've certainly enjoyed telling it!

Blessings,

Dr. Paulette Clark

EMPOWERING THE ENTREPRENEUR WITHIN

Ebony Archer

*I*n life, each of us will encounter many challenging times. The trials and tribulations we face will often try to discourage us and will cause us to lose hope in ourselves and in the goals we want to achieve in life. For me, one of those goals was to become an entrepreneur, specifically a business owner who could who could positively impact the lives of others. I often thought of this goal as a challenge due to lack of finances. Growing up, I'd suffered through extreme poverty and even homelessness. At times, I felt like a victim of my own circumstances.

At the age of eighteen, I was working three jobs, attending college, and trying to build my business on the side. It was not easy. As a matter of fact, it was challenging. I had come from a family who'd taught me to just get a good education and a good job; they had never really supported the idea of going into business for myself, being in control of my own income, which was what I really wanted to do. Despite the challenges, setbacks, and trials I'd faced in life, I realized that I had to empower the entrepreneur within.

Strangely enough, every challenge we face or any obstacle we are forced to overcome can be an inspiration, something that shapes us into the person God has chosen us to be. Every experience, emotion, and challenge we encounter should be a motivator; it is our responsibility to learn from these and keep striving toward a brighter future. Truly, one's determination leads to one's destination. Let life inspire you! Don't give up, and always keep the faith. In order to succeed in life, we must first believe in ourselves, because with the Father on our side, there is nothing we cannot do.

Right now, many individuals are eager to step out into the path of entrepreneurship, but far too many are stopped by fear. Understand that fear is an excuse that will prevent you from achieving what you want in life. I admit that becoming an entrepreneur is a daunting task. Why? Because every sole decision relies on you. The source of your income is dependent on the actions you take, and your efforts will directly determine how successful you are.

Some are not fearful of stepping into entrepreneurship, but they do not know where to start. So many ask, "How do I become an entrepreneur?" I could list the step-by-step strategies to becoming a successful entrepreneur, but at the end of the day, if you do not believe in yourself and in the business you want to start, you are ultimately setting yourself up for failure. I am happy to share with you, however, three lessons I have learned about becoming an entrepreneur and keeping that business growing:

Self-belief is the key to your destiny.

Doubt and the lack of belief were two factors that hindered me from moving forward as entrepreneur. Why? Because I believed others' opinions. I allowed myself to see things from their perspective, their point of view instead of my own. I took in the words they said and allowed that to dictate me and my actions.

Finally, a realization came to me, and I asked myself, How did I get to this point? I wasn't happy at all because I was not fulfilling the path that was set out for me. I believed in everyone else but not in myself. I knew this had to change, so I worked hard to develop a sense of self-belief. This gave me the confidence to finally start my business.

There is power in self-belief because it is the fuel you need to keep going, keep striving, keep reaching for success. As entrepreneurs, self-belief must be a foundation of our businesses, and a business built on this type of confidence has a much better chance of still standing in the end.

Don't just write the vision. Speak it!

After I gained the confidence to start my business, I was then ready for the next step, which was to write out my vision. Even after I wrote it down, though, things did not progress as I expected; nothing seemed to be happening. I began to fall into a deep depression until I recalled an old, wise saying: "Speak it and it shall be so." When you speak something into the atmosphere, speak it into existence or into the universe, your actions will begin to follow what your voice says. With this in mind, every morning before I start my day, I read my vision out loud to myself, like a mantra, repeating it over and over again. Speaking my vision helped me really, truly believe in it.

I challenge you, as an entrepreneur, to set aside time each and every day to speak aloud your vision for your business. Speak into existence the goals and financial status you want your business to achieve, for in order to believe it, you have to speak it.

Empower yourself daily.

As an entrepreneur, I had to learn that I needed to empower myself daily. Why? Entrepreneurs face many challenges and much opposition, and we must make many sacrifices. These are the very reasons why so many entrepreneurs are so quick to give up, but there are some methods to help you overcome this and stay empowered.

First, start each day with a positive quote. Your day will be centered on your early thoughts. If you start off thinking positively, you will likely see more positive results from your actions that day.

Second, surround yourself with people who are in similar situations, entrepreneurs with a positive attitude. You will see that you are not walking this road of entrepreneurship alone, and you will be empowered by the success of others.

Track your progress.

I learned to track my progress in my business because it helps to see when goals are being accomplished and my vision is being fulfilled. This gives me the extra push I needed to continue to believe in my business.

After reading this, you may ask, "Why is self-empowerment so important?" Self-empowerment is important because *you* are the foundation of your business. If you do not empower or believe in yourself, your business will always be stagnant. Your first step to becoming successful must be to empower the entrepreneur within!

FROM SIX FIGURES TO ZERO

Dr. Renee Sunday

*"G*ood day, Dr. Renee Sunday. We do not need your services anymore."

This was what Dr. Renee Sunday was told almost two years ago. She went from six figures to zero in one single day, just twenty-four short hours, and she was forced to make a decision to move beyond that difficult situation. It's no mystery that losing her job caused serious effects on her life in many aspects, but it still was not an excuse to give up. Instead, Renee uncovered simple, life-changing strategies to rely on during that difficult season of her life: believe, trust, and move forward.

First, Dr. Renee Sunday simply took some time to reflect on what had occurred. Yes, she lost her prestigious and well-paying position. Was it because several companies needed to let go of several employees due to necessary pay cuts, or could it have been more personal? Maybe her employer felt Renee's contributions were not appropriate for the position. Whether she villainized her ex-employer or allowed herself to feel like a victim, the point was that something just wasn't working. Renee considered that it may not have been the most suitable position for her. She reevaluated her strengths, weaknesses, and passions. *Maybe I just wasn't passionate about the work I was doing,* she thought, *or maybe it just didn't fit with my purpose in this crossroad of life.* She spent much time reflecting, considering what really happened and dissecting her feelings about it. Once Renee's mind was a little clearer, she was ready to move forward with intentionality, power, and tenacity. She knew what type of work she was interested in pursuing, based on her strengths and passions.

Meanwhile, Renee took some precise actions at home to help maintain her happiness and lifestyle while the new season was being birthed. She continued to pay bills and fulfill her responsibilities, balancing that with a bit of leisure spending. Renee didn't have a streamlined budget, but she knew it was the perfect time for her to create one, a great opportunity to rework her expenses. She made several cutbacks of her own. Eating out was the biggest one; now she cooks healthy, gourmet meals on a daily basis. Striking a balance between her financial obligations and her happiness and emotional wellbeing was a process, and she knew things would work out in the end.

The key to her emotional state was the inner voice and peace that came from within. Renee's journey to fulfilling her dreams and purpose was always positive, vivid, and close to her heart and mind. She made sure to surround herself with likeminded people, and doubt and unbelief never entered her mind. It was a crossroads, a chance to start over. At times, it felt daunting, scary, nerve-racking, and stressful, but it was as a beautiful opportunity, a blessing in disguise. Positive that she would rise again, Renee focused on the joys of life: God, family, and friends.

It was the perfect time to take some extra walks, go for a swim, take a hike, and even work at home. Renee developed several de-stressing routines. She freed her life from clutter and learned which tasks kept her happy and focused.

The more Renee de-stressed, the more the fulfillment she found in creating and achieving new goals and dreams. She initiated strategies to help her be healthier and happier, balancing priorities and taking positive, steady action. As she achieved smaller goals, bigger ones came to light, and celebration was in the air.

Soon, Renee learned to have patience with herself. She realized her success and happiness would be a lifelong journey, and she took small, consistent steps toward a new and exciting life full of passion, love, and happiness.

She sensed a new season, the next opportunity to soar, the next opened door. She leveraged her skill set to regain zeal and an appreciation for life. Renee evolved into media, journalism, and assisting others through difficult situations. In time, her experience propelled her to an overflowing, more abundant life filled with joy unspeakable. Dr. Renee Sunday's experience revitalized, rebuilt, and renewed her! She allowed the process to mold and shape her into a wonderfully made diamond that now shines with excitement, joy, and love.

THE BENEFITS OF LOSING YOUR J.O.B

*B*esides the obvious—juggling overdue bills because you are just over broke—there is a financial gift waiting for you at the end of the tunnel. Most people who start their own business are not aware of the many benefits they can enjoy just by owning life as an entrepreneur.

Many small businesses qualify for tax breaks, especially if you work from your home.[1] The IRS states that your home office can be a separate room, but it does not have to be. In fact, it must only be a "separately identifiable space," and permanent partitions are not necessary to mark off that space. If you do not have permanent partitions, you should take care to define the space with furniture or some other way, because you must only use this space for business purposes.

The key in taking the home office deduction is that the office space must not be for both personal and business use. If you want to use your home office space as a deduction, it shouldn't be the same place where you pay your bills, host a game of spades, entertain your children, or surf the web and email friends.

---

1   www.irs.gov

Also, it must be used regularly for business, so "incidental or occasional business use" does not qualify. Some exceptions to exclusive use apply for licensed daycare owners and those who store inventory in their home. My suggestion for any new  business owner is to thoroughly read and understand IRS Publication 587, or consult a tax specialist to ensure that you are in compliance.

Many variables may prevent you from claiming tax write-offs. Be very leery of any get-rich-by-working-at-home schemes, because they may become more expensive than what you can feasibly claim.

In addition to tax write-offs, another great benefit is the freedom to be your own boss! Many people can handle this responsibility like a champ, while others need a little coaching. If you are not used to structuring your time, a mindset coach may be a great investment, as it will teach you how to focus and command your day to maximize your efforts and become successful in your business venture.

While you are being coached or practicing what you already know, you will quickly see that hard work does, indeed, pay off. You will be able to spend time with those you love, the people who truly make you happy. You can enjoy little league games and recitals and attend doc-  tor visits for you and your family—all things that are vital to your emotional and physical wellbeing.

What worked for me was to write a schedule of the things I needed to do and the things I *wanted* to do. Once your priorities are set, any free time can be dedicated to rest, family, and some leisure. It is all about balance.

EMPLOYMENT TKO

DON'T GET KNOCKED OUT!!

TKO *Noun* \ ˌtē-ˌkā-ˈō\
Technical knockout
First Known Use: 1941

*T*here are three dates I will never forget, because my entire life shifted on those days, changing how I viewed my circumstances. Naturally, losing a job was a life-changing event, especially since I had little ones to provide for. I cringed when a bill was due, and it was so nerve-racking to even switch the lights on. Some months, it required a creative story to get them back on. *How did it get to this point?* I wondered. *How could a well-educated, college woman with multiple certifications and credentials plummet to this state of lack?* It was the result of a technical knockout, an employment TKO, the result of a real sucker punch.

It started when I moved to Delaware; it was supposed to have been a euphoric experience, one that would yield a much-coveted fairytale ending: the kids, the three-quarter-acre back yard, and a beautiful home. I was an entrepreneur, and I was on my way—or so I thought.

It seemed to be a picture-perfect situation; however, I didn't really own the keys to the house, the beautiful yard, and all those amenities and luxuries. Most of the time, I had a nice bank account, but the lack of savings and my desire for grandeur, always wanting the best, took precedence over my sense of good judgment. Living in a 3,000-square-foot home required me to look swank, to have all jewels and clothes that the world regarded as the finer things in life. It didn't take long before the commas in my bank account started moving over unfavorably for me, and I found myself counting pennies, wondering how to make the last $7,000 stretch.

I was not working my business at all, nor was I reading or learning about others who'd been successful in the industry where I'd hoped to prosper. I began to get sidetracked and distracted, and I knew I had to do something and do it quick. I eventually moved into my own house; truth be told, I was not adding value to the situation I was in, and I had to make that change.

As is the case for most people who want to reinvent themselves, I had to do some real soul-searching and ask myself what I wanted to do outside of substance abuse treatment. I was sure there had to be something I would love to do, something that would pay the bills and fulfill me at the same time. I'd finally found my identity in a great industry, and it afforded me a life that I loved. Again I let my guard down and trusted, and I failed to remain focused. The number-one rule for any entrepreneur is to stay focused and on point at all times.

Needless to say, the situation was tragic and demeaning. Have you ever been in a situation where even underground would not be deep enough to hide? I was at my all-time low and needed to take the phoenix route, to rise from the flames instead of burying my head like an ostrich and copping out. I was now forced to get a traditional job and make ends meet, and it wasn't easy to make sense of it all.

It was almost as if I'd forgotten how to fill out applications. *Am I really that far removed?* I had to ask myself. *I finally found something that spoke to my passion, working with those who needed motivation to persevere, to stay alive. Yes!* I thought. *I can do this. I'll be great in this clinical field, especially since I've had experience in it for years.* I landed the job on my first interview; the second interview literally took place on my first day on the job. I started two days before my birthday, and it seemed as if it was going to be a great job. I had a huge, cushy office with a nice view of the city, a mid-level position and with a great benefits package. I was riding high while observing the phony agency relationships fold and unfold on a daily basis right before my eyes.

I was never one to involve myself with any clique, nor do I gossip and backbite, so I kept to myself until I was approached being stand-offish. Anyone who knows me will tell you I am certainly the complete opposite of that; however, I let it go, because there was yet another office war going on and I wanted no part of it. As the snowball effect would have it, the entire staff was restructured, as well as the grant for which we were all competing.

I vividly remember how happy everyone was that the grant was on its way, and we were ready to celebrate just for being considered. I didn't go out with the crew that night, so I missed the memo, so to speak, about the changes coming up the pike. I went to work as usual and received a phone call from one of my many clients; he had suicidal ideations and was thinking of a plan to, as he put it, "end it all." Of course I asked the necessary questions to assess his situation, and then directed him to 911. When he called back, he had given up on his termination plan, but he was heavily depressed. I spoke to him for a while and did what I could to defuse the situation. He thanked me for talking him "off of the cliff" and said he was on his way to my office to update his service plan and research psychologist in the area. I felt really good and was happy that it was a happy ending, at least for him.

Almost as soon as I got off the phone, my supervisor asked me to see her in the director's office for a quick meeting. Since she'd been in my office for most of the conversation with the client, I assumed she wanted to talk to me about that successful call. She had even given me a high-five and kudos for a job well done. I even considered she might want to see me about a raise; salary inspections were underway, and there was the new grant to think about.

After spending about eight minutes to tell me how good of a job I'd done, they rewarded me with a pink slip instead of a raise. Of course the director told me it was the company and not me, but my face must have said it all, because my direct supervisor got up and moved away, just in case I threw a chair or a punch. On the contrary, for some reason, I felt as if a huge load had been lifted from my soul. I was quickly sent on my way, with a severance check and my belongings, including a potted plant. That cardboard box held my dreams: my babies going to college, vacations, my house, my car, and my retirement. Just like that, all those dreams and aspirations were left on the second floor of the Community Building, and I was forced to move on to the next chapter of my life.

"See ya tomorrow, Ms. Sean. Have a great day," the parking attendant said.

As I drove off, all I could do is smile and sigh. It was as if a film of muck had been lifted off of me, and I felt free. I felt invincible, and every care, heartbreak, and disappointment was gone from my spirit by the time I got home. I spent the next three days soul-searching and examining myself to see who I was and where I wanted to go. I knew being unemployed was not what I wanted.

Three days later, I got a call from an agency I'd interviewed with months prior, and they offered me better pay and a start date. I was so excited, and just that quick, I forgot about my promise to myself, my revelation that it was time for me to write a book, to start my coaching and motivational speaking business. I used the excuse of what people were saying about me, as opposed to the gift I've been blessed with. I felt like Public Enemy No. 1, and I had somewhat of a bad reputation, so I was sure no one would want to hear anything from me. With that in mind, back to a J.O.B. I went.

The first six months was like a dream come true. I immediately took on a leadership role and got in good with my higher-ups. My clients were awesome, and I felt great, but then life happened again. My schedule was switched around due to changes in staffing and the needs of the clients. I went from facilitating two groups to four, and all those extra hours were creeping up on me. Soon, it was not at all the shiny path I'd thought it was, but I am a fighter and was loyal to my employers; I would not let my feelings show—especially since I was told that help was on the way and that the three open staff lines would soon be filled. We were supposed to manage forty to fifty-five coed clients; however, my caseload peaked at seventy-seven. Anyone in social services will realize this is an unmanageable number, especially when there are forty-five-minute one-on-one sessions, note documentation, four groups, and supervision to deal with. It just didn't seem possible, nor did it seem right.

Time went on, and seventy-seven clients later, I was sent on a three-day training session to enhance; it was assumed that I would be a much better clinician and be able to better service my clients with impeccable knowledge and understanding of the tools that would equip me to be the best of the best. In the end, I found myself in the unemployment office with the certificates from the state. Who gets let go while they are at agency-paid training? This girl! Once again, the hiatus between unemployment and gainful employment seemed like an eternity.

Meanwhile, my now-ex told me that I had to be out of his house within an unreasonable amount of time because he would not be able to carry me and my kids. The man I'd hoped would put a ring on it simply gave me the boot instead. It was rough to try to fulfill my dreams, earn income, and look for a place all at the same time, especially when I lost my car over a so-called clerical error. The running joke is that I tried everything from Amway to Zamzuu, but there were no magic get-rich-quick pills or potions. I even tried selling Rainbows Vacuums, tutoring ESL students, restarting a stale Mary Kay business, all to no avail, and time was ticking.

Finally, I caught a break when Lisa, a dear friend of mine, told me about a realtor who would look at my character more than my circumstances. Much to my delight, she found a place I was able to afford, and everything seemed to fall into place after that. I got my house, car, and a job all within a week, and I thought—once again—that I had arrived, until the pain started to override the pleasure.

I wasn't sure what made me think another J.O.B. would be better than the situation I'd been in with Ardyss. Maybe it was because the money did not come in a form of a check every other week, or maybe I missed the office life. I can honestly say the only remunerative endeavor I enjoyed was at Ardyss International. The income I was blessed with from Ardyss came on time, and it sustained me until I was hit with another knockout.

I went to back to the abuse, the neglect, and the old ball-and-chain from eleven a.m. to nine p.m. I missed so much of my kids' lives because I could not afford to take time off. God forbid if I took ten extra minutes on a break or lunch; a message from the owner to my supervisor would be guaranteed, the same old speech about responsibility and a reminder that time is money. Of course I knew those things, but when one is only allotted enough time to heat up a little food and walk back to one's cubicle, it makes for a little time spillage. Also, top producers should be given a little leeway.

The accounts manager saw the microscopic hole in the needle of management and gave his notice. Once that happened, all Hades broke loose; it was every man or woman for themselves once the owner took over. He gave his marching orders and changed around a system that 1) he did not know how to navigate and 2) had been working just fine. We were above productivity level, yet even that was not enough. He even demanded that all cell phones be placed in a box upon the start of our shift; even personal emergencies would have to wait until four to six p.m. to be addressed. It was complete insanity, but I needed a check and needed one bad.

I began to realize, though, that I had not attended a great university, only to be hazed like that at my place of employment. It was totally unacceptable, and it needed to be stopped fast. My fed-up moment was when my check was 30 percent short for the second time, without so much as an explanation or an apology. Needless to say, I did not return after that weekend. I had had enough. Little did I know that the ultimate knockout was swiftly on its way.

Who gets into a tragic car accident the same day when they're laid off from the job at which they grossed over $99,000 in revenue within four months? This girl! Feel free to insert a long, dramatic eye-roll here, but while you're doing that, allow me to backtrack and tell the story.

I left the field of health and human services because it became too stressful. The hours were long, and the only passion I had for the job was for the paycheck. I eventually found myself stretching borrowed money, because my pay simply was not enough to cover my bills and life aside. I rationed funds and was a good steward of my money, but the ends kept barely missing each other. I dug through job boards, but even opportunities that offered six figures told me I was over qualified or that I had the experience but was just missing a specific credential. So, when I saw a semi-decent opportunity, I had to go for it. I was hired immediately, and the bell sounded for the last round.

I had landed a blue-collar job, and I had a hard time transitioning from heels to boots. The hours were long, but the money was longer; my weekly checks covered 90 percent of my expenses. I was so excited because I felt financially free. Bills were paid early, with money left over for savings. I began to enjoy the quality of life I was used to. This went on for several months, as I received corporate recognition, awards, bonuses, trips, etc. It was all good until the bottom fell out.

I knew things were growing bleak when half of our team received pink slips, and I was the last of eight standing in our regional division. My supervisor, as cool as he was, fought the water in his eyes when he had to tell me it was a wrap, due to the seasonal layoffs. I was a no longer the same commodity they'd raved about, and they were willing to let me go.

I wondered what happened to all the bells and whistles, to all those praises they'd been singing about me. All of that had been replaced with, "See you next year," and a condescending bit of advice I did not need: "Be sure to allocate your money appropriately." I felt as if I was being "punked", but there were no cameras around. I felt a pit in my stomach at first, but that soon turned into trust and euphoric joy. I skipped out with plans to go to the unemployment office, then to the house to scoop up my kids for practice.

All went well and was peaceful; I had plans to finish my first book and then release this and the other. Goals and visions began to populate in my mind, and I determined that all would be well and that I would survive. Those were the last thoughts in my mind when practice for my kids let out. It began to rain, so I directed my kids to stay inside and wait for me to avoid getting wet. I was glad for that, because as soon as I got in my van and pulled out of my spot to swing around and get them, SMACK!

As I lay on the gurney inside the ambulance, I watched my life flash by, and I heard my kids screaming and crying for me. If I get another chance, I thought, I have to do this right. I had to ensure that a collection plate would not have to go around covering any expenses for me. My debts needed to be paid, and I did not know how I was going to pull that off while I was laid up in the hospital or at home.

That was when it really hit me: I was working hard to fuel someone else's dream while my own lay dormant, on life support and barely holding on. It did not seem like a smart situation, and I'd already given up over 5,000 hours of my life that I would never get back, a sacrifice that ended in an employment TKO. I had missed recitals, games, baby teeth falling out, and other milestones in my children's lives, and no paycheck, bonus, or incentive could ever replace those precious moments.

Today, I am my own boss, and I love it. Is it hard work? Absolutely! However, I work and live on my own terms, and I have become a better mother to my children. The babysitter is now employed on an as-needed basis rather than raising my babies and making decisions on my behalf because of my work schedule.

I now run and operate Awake the Champion in You Ministries, which provides volunteer community outreach for those who are dealing with substance abuse, homelessness, HIV, cancer, abuse, and at-risk situations. We also reach out to sex offenders and gang members. In addition, we consult companies seeking to increase their vision and revenue. It's somewhat like a train-the-trainer concept, delving deep into their mission statement and regenerating the staff. We also have an elite, professional speaking division, recruited by companies, churches, schools, and jails to motivate, enhance, and promote positive change in people's lives. Please visit www.awakethechampioninyou.org to learn more about our mission and vision. Ultimately, our goal is to provide transitional housing for veterans, women, children, and ex-offenders, and with an extra 5,000 hours and a good group of people in my corner, all of it is possible!

What I've learned from my journey is this: People will only do to you what you allow them to. It's time to quit the 40/40/40 Club and open your own shop so you can truly enjoy the ride. Do not enter entrepreneurship seeking to get rich, because that seldom happens, but if you seek change and improvements, hoping to eliminate an area of lack or enhance a dynamic, the money will come.

Also seek wise counsel and budget your books. I cannot say that enough. Budget your books! Being the biggest fish in the pond is a fruitless situation; however, when you surround yourself around those who learn from you, those you learn from, and those you learn with, your world will expand, and blessings will flow around you. My name is LaSean Rinique, and I had an employment TKO that sparked my journey to change.

I CAN'T QUIT

Mia Zachary

*L*osing your job is scary and depressing. Getting fired is shocking and humiliating. Either way, being unemployed sucks, and it's common—at least at first—to feel some resentment. Still, after the dust has settled and the tears have dried, you can and should take a long, hard look in the mirror…and smile!

You might have lost something important, but in the process, you gained something essential: an opportunity to forge a better path, one that will lead to happiness, fulfillment, and the enrichment of others.

I'm writing this essay from the comfort of my nice, warm bed. Why? Because I can. As an entrepreneur, I've got the freedom to **#DesignMyLife**, not just make a living. I set my own hours, make my own schedule, decide who I will or won't work with and choose which projects to take on, and how much money I make directly depends on how hard I'm willing to work. I don't have to wait for my boss to give permission or approval for days off or pay raises.

It wasn't always like this though.

I've been employed as a retail salesclerk, a receptionist, a bookseller, a paralegal, and an office manager. However, in spite of all those J.O.B.s, I've always been an entrepreneur at heart. I'm a best-selling fiction novelist, and full-time writing is a personal business. I incorporated and ran my own publishing company, until I realized I was keeping it afloat with my credit cards. I started a romantic getaways travel agency, before September 11 tanked the tourism industry in 2001. And through it all, I've worked as a creative vision developer/coach and freelance editor.

My longest traditional employment was as a workers' compensation paralegal. I worked ten years for the same firm. Ten years! I blame television. The female attorney on *Hill Street Blues* was such a brilliant, beautiful role model. *L.A. Law* made the legal field look so sexy, fun, and cool, and don't even get me started on holiday weekend marathons of *Law & Order*!

Reality, though, can never compare to Hollywood.

I have four tattoos: two are Japanese kanji, meaning "new moon" and "water" respectively; one is a butterfly; and the other is a phoenix. In case you can't tell from the symbols I have chosen to permanently mark on my body, I do not handle tiny, windowless cubicles very well at all. I won't give the real name of the firm; I'll just use "SB&S" because. Trust me when I say there was a whole lot of BS about that environment.

I was miserable, and I quickly grew to hate my paralegal job—so much so that I could barely get out of bed in the morning. I walked into the building every day, muttering under my breath, "This is not my real life. This is not my real life," all the way down the hall, up the elevator, and to my desk. Despite the fact that I'd made a couple good friends from among my co-workers, I despised every second I had to be there.

So why didn't I just quit? I tried, sort of. I wanted to, but I couldn't just quit without the promise of another source of income. There were also elements of fear, pride, and commitment. I didn't want to let anyone down: my supervisor, my family, or myself. I hate the very idea of being a quitter!

Still, I spent a lot of hours looking for other jobs and was even invited to a couple interviews. In hindsight, I realize those prospective employers probably saw my secret: I didn't really want to work for them any more than I wanted to work at the job I already held.

Steve Jobs said, "Sometimes life hits you in the head with a brick." My brick came in the shape of an HR manager by the name of Karen. It was a typical, late-in-the-day, end-of-the-week office visit, except that

I'd just returned from a week of bereavement after the death of my father. Let me tell you, #ThatWasAMonday! Even after getting fired, though, I had to do things my own way. I got another paralegal to cover my cases for the next day and quickly sorted my other cases that had upcoming hearings.

As I put my few belongings into a small box (I've never brought many personal items to work, as that makes it all the easier to leave), I kept a fairly sober expression on my face. However, I wasn't thinking about my reputation or their references. I walked out of the building, into the sunlight of the summer afternoon, with a huge grin on my face, and a weight lifted from my shoulders. Over and over in my mind, I thought, *Thank you, God! I am so relieved!*

The next week or so was spent catching up on sleep and movies, while my brothers encouraged me to update my résumé and get another paralegal job. What followed was a little soul-searching and a lot of personal transformation. I should have been making a certain amount of money, should have gotten myself promoted to a brag-worthy position, should have whatever. Over the following weeks, money became tight, and times were kind of tough, but **trying times are times for trying harder**.

Life is too short. Why do something you hate? Nobody else's idea of success is the same as mine. *I* have to decide what it means to me and for me. Comparing paths with others is nothing but a recipe for self-sabotage. So when I go to work, it's *my* work.

I got a crazy idea one afternoon while drafting a new book manuscript and that turned into my first trademarked invention, the Writing Blocks Idea Dice® (rebranded in 2013 as Noodle Cubes™). I penned two nonfiction books on the craft of plotting, *Story Building Solutions* and *The Ultimate Idea Factory*. I turned the second book into a workshop for kids and the first into a weekend-long intensive fiction writing master class called, "From Mind…To Manuscript!"™.

Along the way, I met an incredible man, Glenn Garnes, who become my business mentor and evolved into a treasured friend. Glenn, a former lawyer who has been an entrepreneur for over a decade, often says, "I love what I do because I love chosen to #DoWhatILove." So, when he invited me to be part of a new venture with him, I didn't hesitate.

Becoming a founding member of Small Business CEO CoLabs in Laurel, Maryland, was honestly the smartest decision I've ever made. I've had so many great experiences, have met a lot of incredible, positive people, and I can't wait to get to work on the days I'm at CoLabs. This purpose-driven, unified office space is populated with entrepreneurs who often brainstorm, mastermind, and collaborate on projects.

At this point, I'd love to tell you about filling my bathtub with $100 bills and swimming in cash, but I believe in being transparently authentic. Entrepreneurship isn't easy, nor is it the path to overnight success. For the most part, entrepreneurs work twice as many hours as traditional employees, often without regular pay or benefits or good sleep or a lunch break, let alone a vacation. For these reasons, entrepreneurship is not for everyone.

If you've been dreaming of leaving your J.O.B., of running your own business, I encourage you to take a chance on your dreams, but in good conscience, I must also advise that you don't start a business to make money. Instead, start to make a difference. Be sure that what you do positively impacts the people around you: your family, your neighborhood, your community, and the world.

I'm currently developing "From Mind…To Manuscript!"™ into a full course for a private high school so teenagers can experience completing their very own novel. I'm creating a signature presentation on depression, with the intention of giving hope from my own experiences. With the encouragement and support of my fellow CoLabs members, my "Cre8ivity Unleashed" workshop is now being restructured as a series of interactive seminars for college-bound teens. None of the projects I have planned for this year and the years to come would be possible if I were still trading time for dollars in my windowless cubicle at the law firm.

As human beings, we all learn from experience. The experience of getting fired from SB&S was the best thing that ever could have happened to me. That led me to take a risk, to take a chance on myself and follow my dream of being a full-time creativity coach/ghost writer/ editor/workshop facilitator/ inventor/web series host/personal development speaker/fiction author. And for that, I am truly, deeply, and eternally grateful.

"You've got to find what you love. And that is as true for your work as it is for your lovers. Your work is going to fill a large part of your life, and the only way to be truly satisfied is to do what you believe is great work. And the only way to do great work is to love what you do. If you haven't found it yet, keep looking. #Don'tSettle. As with all matters of the heart, you'll know when you find it." ~ Steve Jobs

Ms. Zachary is a best-selling author of ten books to date, the trademarked inventor of Noodle Cubes™ idea dice, an innovative tool for sparking "creativity anywhere, every time," and the developer of "From Mind…To Manuscript"™, an interactive workshop that guides participants from a story idea to a first draft in just two days, as well as Entrepubbing™, the first system for entrepreneurs to write a business book in about forty-eight hours. Mia believes your success is in your story and that everyone is the creative type. She can be reached at 702-763-CRE8 and via email at mia@cre8ivity3.com

MY ENTREPRENEURIAL JOURNEY TO MY PASSION AND PURPOSE

Felicia Meadows

*M*y famous phrase lately is, "I've been an entrepreneur in spirit since I was a teenager and an entrepreneur in action for the past few years." While other young people were reading coming-of-age novels, I was picking up books like Dennis Kimbro's *Think and Grow Rich* and *The Mis-Education of the Negro*, by Carter Godwin Woodson. I read any and every piece of motivational, educational, and inspirational material I could get my hands on. I studied entrepreneurship by reading books and attending every workshop that came across my path. I was determined at an early age that I wanted to be my own boss and be wealthy.

My first moneymaking venture was at thirteen, when I started collecting aluminum cans to convert into cash at the recycling center. I picked them up around the neighborhood, at home, and any other place where I could find them. Then, every Saturday, I dragged extra-large trash bags filled with cans to the recycling center to cash in for about five cents on the dollar. After about my third trip to the recycling center and leaving with a miniscule amount of cash for my hard labor, I decided to rethink my business plan.

My next venture was babysitting. I posted an ad in the community newsletter, received numerous phone calls, and got my first assignment within a week. That was short-lived, however. When I took a babysitting job to look after three little boys whose mom worked a nine-hour shift at Bob's Big Boys, I tried for several hours to entertain the two-, three-, and five-year-old as best as a thirteen-year-old could, with my own mother's help. Even though I was overwhelmed by that assignment, my love for children kept me moving in the childcare direction. I started posting little yellow postcards on the "Help Wanted" boards at the grocery store, though it didn't prove successful. After several months with no prospective babysitting gigs, I called it quits.

A few years passed, but the entrepreneurial blood was still flowing through my veins. Armed with a bit of information, I attempted to go to car auctions to make money by buying cars wholesale and flipping them to make more money. However, I wasn't fortunate enough to win any bids; I was not able to outbid people who had significant money to invest. I even went to estate auctions in the hopes of finding the big-ticket item that would catapult my entrepreneurial pursuits to the top. Again, I met with no success.

I must add that while my parents were always supportive of me through my many business ventures, they never really nurtured my entrepreneurial spirit. I was left to my own devices to try to figure out this thing called entrepreneurship.

As the years passed, I ventured out to try even more entrepreneurial endeavors. Having enjoyed the creativity of doing hair and makeup throughout high school, I wanted to become a cosmetologist. After realizing that my parents would not support that dream (college was the only acceptable route for them), I began to research the cost of pursuing it. Since I would be footing the expense myself, I took out a loan to go to cosmetology school to become a manicurist; it was far cheaper. I earned my manicurist license on the first attempt, and I set up shop in the one-room apartment. I had a steady flow of friends and referrals.

My first real business venture was called Flytality, and I partnered with one of my girlfriends, a clothing designer. I was the nail artist, and she was the fashion guru, and our tagline was, "Fashion and nails with a fly mentality." I realized nails were not my passion though.

While I was learning the art of the manicure, I also paid for classes at H&R Block and prepared taxes in the hopes of turning it into a marketable skill that I could work on my own. After incurring over $1,000 in debt to train as a manicurist and hundreds of dollars in industry training, that profession was defunct within two years. My stint as a tax preparer lasted about that long as well.

It is somewhat of a long-running joke that I am a bit of a professional student. Always looking for ways to educate myself, I took countless classes and seminars. While on my search for the ultimate business plan, I continued to pursue higher education. Although I changed my major three times, in 1996, I quit my job and went back to school full time to complete my psychology degree. I only had three semesters left to complete my bachelor's. It was the best decision I ever could have made; I had fallen in love with psychology when I took a general psych course as a high school senior, and ever since I was young, I'd had a gift for analyzing people and helping them find solutions for their various life dilemmas. Combining that gift with my passion for children, I decided to become a school counselor.

In 1998, I finished my undergraduate degree and went through to complete my master's, and I have never looked back. I got my first official job in education in 1998, teaching first grade at a charter school. When I saw all the psychology needs of my babies, I decided that I wasn't best suited to be in the classroom, that I could serve better elsewhere, and I wanted to pursue my passion of psychology.

One day, while perusing the "Jobs" section of *The Washington Post*, I saw the ideal job, a school-to-career counselor with DC Public Schools (DCPS). It was my opportunity to help young people understand their talents, skills, and abilities so they could find suitable careers. Still an entrepreneur in spirit, I became a NFTE certified teacher through Georgetown University while working for the public school system. My hope was to eventually teach entrepreneurship classes to students; however, my tenure with DCPS was short-lived. After completing my master's, I began working as a school counselor at an alternative high school that closed within months, due to internal mismanagement. In 2002, I began working as a school counselor for Prince George's County Public Schools.

I'd been working in my dream job as a school counselor for years, and I could not think of anything else I would rather do. Still, even though I felt I'd found my dream job, the reality of the limited income started to set in. As most people know, educators are overworked and underpaid. Initially, I was able to sustain myself and supplement my income by working afterschool programs and taking on additional duties. However, when funding dried up, so did the opportunities.

I took another major hit in 2010, when the eleven-month position I'd been granted two years prior was snatched out from under me. When the county I work for converted all the counseling positions back to ten months, I took a $7,000 pay cut. Not only that, but over the next four years, no one received a pay raise of any sort, not even a cost-of-living increase. To make matters worse, the state increased our retirement contribution and taxes and raised our medical premiums. Despite education being in utter turmoil, with more students than ever in need of counseling services, my job was on the chopping block. Unbelievably, the county I work for planned to eliminate all school counselors. Somehow, funding was found, and although I didn't lose my job, the fear of had me rethinking my profession and security.

The last straw was the elimination of my position at the school where I'd been assigned for eleven years. Not only did I feel devalued, but this also validated the need for me to truly start my entrepreneurial journey. While I was placed in another school, my dissatisfaction with the state of education, combined with the desire to reach more students, led me want to work with young people in a different capacity. I had worked at every grade level, from elementary to high school, and I suddenly realized that every experience I'd had up to that point had led me to my current field, coaching and consulting.

While working, I still tried to pursue entrepreneurship and wealth. In 2006, I joined 5Linx because I was so impressed with the innovative technology. Unfortunately, I had a horrible experience with the upline I came in under, who was and is continuing to do extremely well in the business. After dropping $500, I was pretty much left to figure the business out on my own. I attended the in-person events and all the conference calls. When I asked my upline for assistance on growing my business, I was given the cold shoulder. I even flew to Atlanta, only to be shunned and ignored the whole time by the very upline who had insisted that I attend the event. Needless to say, the second I got home, I dropped out of the company.

My next multi-level marketing (MLM) experience was a few years later, with Legal Shield. One of my colleagues talked me into joining, and while I saw the benefit of the products and services, I had no interest in peddling them to other people. That was short-lived as well. Not long after that, I joined Mary Kay, because my daughters' grandmother is a representative, and I thought it would be cool to help her out. Unfortunately, since I really had no passion for it, no interest in selling makeup, I made very little money from it. The bottom line is that MLMs are not for me.

Since I can remember, I have thrived on being independent and going against the status quo. Still, I have always had a high level of consciousness about everything, making sure I do everything with the highest level of expertise as possible. Because of this, some of my like-minded friends and I have coined ourselves "Conscious Rebels." We go against the grain yet remain conscientious about how we show up in our profession. This was how I knew in my heart that entrepreneurship was my calling. Looking back, I realize I wasn't successful in any ventures for which I did not have a true passion.

I should also mention the two t-shirt lines I started, embroidery and silkscreen. I actually still have boxes of tees, in storage so long that they've probably suffered a nasty case of dry rot by now. There was the AVON I tried to sell, boxes and boxes of product and booklets sitting in my living room rather than being sold or distributed. I started to write a book, because as an avid reader and great writer, I thought I was destined to be a published author. I bought *Writer's Digest*, researched publishers, and even looked for editors and agents. In my defense, I did complete seven chapters of a fiction novel, but after weeks of writer's block I shelved that project and left it sitting with the hopes of going back to complete it. I've been to every possible event, seminar, and conference on flipping houses, getting rich through real estate and investment, and investing in stocks and bonds. Despite investing in programs, books, DVDs, and the like, none of it has ever taken off for me because my heart simply wasn't in it.

In 2011, I attended Tori Johnson's "Spark and Hustle" conference in Atlanta, determined to find my niche and discover my entrepreneurial passion. While I made some wonderful contacts at the conference, I still left feeling confused. Discontent with working for the school system and needing a change, I tried to find other avenues to pursue. One of my closest friends suggested that I try coaching, so I forked over a bunch of money to take a coaching course; ultimately, I didn't feel as if coaching was something I really wanted to do.

Truthfully, my passion had always been about children, and my purpose was teaching, helping, and serving, which should have been evident all along. In 2013, I started Tomorrow's Future, which combines coaching with my love for young people and education. As the CEO and founder, my mission is to empower young people to find their own passion and purpose so they can live the life of their dreams. Since beginning that new venture, everything has fallen into place effortlessly. Now that I look back, I realize that all those other attempts at entrepreneurship did not work out because I was not working in my passion or purpose.

In addition to my coaching and consulting business, I plan to open my own charter school by 2018. As an educator, I want young people to have access to quality education that will prepare them for the twenty-first century. The past six months have been phenomenal! I have made some divine connections, participated in professional networking events, and attended conferences that have given me tools and resources to help me grow my business. I've even fulfilled one of my part-time passions, writing, by contributing to two books.

Confucius once said, "Love what you do, and you'll never work a day in your life," and that's exactly what I intend to do!

MAP A PLAN

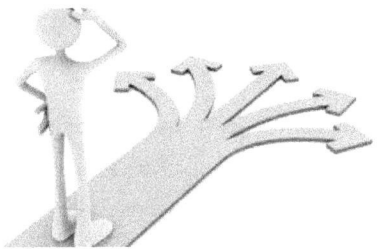

Staying focused is a difficult thing to do if you do not have a plan mapped out. If you are anything like me, you've got fifty tabs opened in your head at one time. I've had to learn to actually write down my plans and my attainable goals. Once one goal is achieved, I move on to the next. Still, this can be challenging for a serial entrepreneur.

Nevertheless, once you have your eyes on the prize, there is absolutely nothing you cannot do! Here is the secret: Once you find your purpose and put a voice to it, do a search on the industry and the leaders who work in it. Read about them from beginning to end and find out what, when, why, where, how, and when they did things. Try to contact them and see if you can intern, or even interview them to see what it takes to be the greatest in that field. Always remember these two things: There is enough money for everyone, and everyone gets their turn.

Once you are sure about your goals and how to reach them, put it all down on paper. So many times, we have wonderful, robust ideas but we never put them into action. Once it is right there in black and white, you have no choice but to tackle it and make it happen.

Identify exactly what need you are satisfying or the desire that you have: *I would like to be viewed as an expert in the motivation field.*

That is a great goal, but how will I do it? What will separate me from all the others in the field? You must state how you will attain this goal, and everyone's answer will be different, depending on the desire; it may also change. For me, it will be: *I, LaSean Rinique, plan to complete a how-to book by December 15, 2014*

I made it personal by adding my name to it, and I made it specific. I did not just say I will write or that I will write every year. Instead, I mentioned detailed action steps to make it happen. Each goal should have a date, something to hold you accountable. Make sure this is feasible, achievable, and reasonable, so you don't set yourself up for failure.

For the first three months, you should incorporate three to five steps. Avoid overwhelming yourself with dozens of them, or you may be compelled to give up too soon: *1) Create subject matter that I am familiar with by June 15, 2014; 2) Create an outline by July 1, 2014; 3) Create a title by July 3, 2014; 4) Buy a domain to own the name by July 3, 2014; and 5) Write three pages per day from July 4 to August 30, 2014.*

Once those action steps are completed, I can add a few more, until the project is actually done, hopefully by the date specified. Again, yours may look different than mine; however, if done properly, you will get the same results: success!

Make sure you do not divert from your plan, and stay grounded, even when it looks like it is not going anywhere. I assure you that you will reach your goal in due time. Studies show that an expert in their field masters their craft within the first three to five years and becomes fully acclaimed within seven to ten years. Don't cut yourself short. Know your worth, and make time count rather than counting time.

Use this time to plan out your success! Below is a simple worksheet that will enable you to delineate a few goals and measure them. If it is not written down, it did not happen, nor will it. You really will benefit by having a living, breathing goals sheet to refer to. From experience, I can tell you it is a mighty good feeling when you can check off a goal on your list and start working on the next one. A word to the wise though: Do not overwhelm yourself by trying to shove a multitude of goals on your plate. Make sure they are realistic, attainable, and measurable. Never leave a goal floating in space without a due date; this will not hold you to the goal, and you will not take it seriously without a deadline.

I also suggest that you find an accountability circle, a group of individuals who are more interested in your improvement than in stroking your ego. These folks will confront and challenge you. They make rock the boat a few times, but the outcomes are always favorable.

My name is _____

and I plan to _____

_____

How will you attain this goal?

I want to _____

because it will _____

_____

What is your timeline for attaining this goal?

I will _____ by_____

What steps will you take to attain this goal? (not too many, don't overwhelm yourself)

1. _____ by _____
2. _____ by _____
3. _____ by _____
4. _____ by _____

My accountability circle includes:

1. _____
2. _____
3. _____
4. _____

LIVING WITHOUT REGRET

Ruben West

"Regret for the things we did can be tempered by time;
it is regret for the things we did not do that is inconsolable."
~ Sidney J. Harris

*H*ow many times have you had an idea for a product or service or maybe even an invention and thought about how great it would be? Then, six months, a year, or maybe even two years later, you see that someone else actually developed that very same product, service, or invention, and you think to yourself, *Man, I already thought of that!* Now it's too late, and someone else is capitalizing on what you thought of years ago.

Having a great idea is common, but what is far less common is taking action on them. As a matter of fact, when I speak, I typically ask my audiences that very question I started with here. Invariably, most everyone has had an idea for a product or service or invention. Furthermore, almost everyone failed to take action, only to see that great idea in the hands of someone else later. Life is funny that way.

Here, I'll tell you how to take action and live without regrets. Most importantly, it's not what you think of; it's what you act on.

Think about this: Thoughts and ideas are energy. As a matter of fact, a single thought can change the way you feel, change your heart rate, and even change your blood pressure. Thoughts can make you feel hunger, excitement, or a wide range of other emotions. Simply put, thoughts are energy. When we look at Newton's Laws of Physics, we learn that energy is never lost and is only transferred. That's exactly what I believe happens to our ideas when we do not act on them. You get the idea and are excited about it for a period of time. Then, once the universe realizes that you are not going to act on it, that idea—that energy—is transferred to someone else, allowing them the opportunity to act on it. This idea or energy may be transferred to thousands of people before someone finally decides to act on it. Then, once it is released, all the thousands of people, you included, who originally had the idea start to regret the fact that they never took action.

Every day, millions of people dream of starting some type of entrepreneurial venture. Their reasons vary from genuine passion and excitement to frustration with their current employer or job situation. For some, it is merely a fleeting thought, and it's probably good that those people do not rush out and start it; the excitement for the idea will only last as long as the emotion. Once the emotion passes or subsides, they will lose interest in the project. The bottom line is: They do not have a strong enough reason to push the project to completion, and it ultimately fails.

I was tested in this very way. My original degree is in criminal justice, with emphasis on juvenile corrections. I remember doing my internship at the County Youth Detention Center in Topeka, Kansas. I recall walking up to the brick building for the first time and as I looked at the tall fence designed to keep the kids in. *I'd hate to live there*, I thought. I guess no one liked living there, but unfortunately, because of choices they had made, many kids did, at least for a time.

After my first week, I had the system down. I recognized all the keys and was aware of all the scheduled activities. I studied the policy manual to gain a deeper understanding of the profession. Still, something was missing. It wasn't shaping up to be what I was expecting.

Think about your current situation. Is it what you thought it would be? Are you living the life you envisioned, or are you caught in a career that fails to meet your expectations? Maybe you're making great money, but you're not making an impact in the lives of others. On the other hand, maybe you're making an impact, but you're suffering financially because your employment does not provide the income needed to live the life you imagined for yourself. Could it be that the profession you are currently in was one you chose many years ago, under different life circumstances, and now it's time for a change?

In my case, I hadn't even graduated, yet I realized the profession I chosen was not shaping up to be nothing like I thought it should be. In my mind, I planned to lead and mentor young kids who may have been somewhat misguided. My days as an intern at the juvenile detention center mostly consisted of saying, "Stop that! Sit down! Line up! Go to you room!" over and over again. Honestly, I was just babysitting, and I had to question why that would require a college degree; my sister was only eleven, and even she had babysitting jobs. I had to figure out what my next step was going to be. I knew I wanted to mentor youth, but there had to be a better way.

Like the situation I was in, you may find yourself at a crossroads. You made a decision on a job or career, but it is not shaping up to be what you need it to be. The question then becomes, "Now what?" Do you go along with the decision you made simply because you made that decision? Do you stay on the same course because you have family and friends who expect you to, or are you willing to look within yourself and ask, *Is this really me? Is this what I was called to do?*"

I decided to look within myself and see how I could use the skills and talents I already had to do what I felt I'd been called to do. *Karate school,* I thought to myself. I had been studying martial arts, and I was sure it would be perfect. As great as the idea sounded at that instant, I immediately started to question how I could possibly own a school, just as we often worry and doubt when we think of that product, service, or invention we talked about earlier. All the responsibilities of marketing and advertising bothered me: *What if I'm not good or experienced enough? What if I can't compete with the established schools around town? Anyway, what do I know about being a business owner?*

Day after day, I tried to talk myself out of the idea, but something kept calling me. Finally, I started to focus on what I had as opposed to what I lacked. The more I thought about it, the more I realized I already had the most important ingredient, the why: *I'll do it for the kids.* Willis Whitney said, "Some men have thousands of reasons why they cannot do what they want to, when all they need is one reason why they can."

There are many reasons why living authentically is important, and avoiding regret is one of them. Life is never going to just hand over to you what you want. You have to be willing to take it. If you have lost your job or you think you may want to lose your job and become an entrepreneur, what do you feel you've been called to do? How can you use your skills and talents to help others? In what way can you make an impact in your community, surrounding area, or globally? Think of it this way: If you can solve big problems, you can make big money; impact drives income.

Not only did I try to talk myself out of starting a martial arts school, but other people did the same. They told me about all the people who had tried and failed. They told me about the risk of people not paying on time, about how the people would drop out of the program. The list went on and on, and—quite frankly—everything they said turned out to be true. Nonetheless, I had the will, drive, and determination to keep pursuing it, regardless of any setbacks I faced.

To date, I've started two martial art schools, both in Topeka. One has been in business for eighteen years, the other for sixteen. Yes, I've faced setbacks and hardships along the way, but I've always had the will to persevere.

Looking back now, after teaching students of all ages, training champion martial artists, and being inducted into the U.S. Martial Arts Hall of Fame in 2005 as Instructor of the Year, I realize that my success was always in my hands. In spite of all the people who told me I couldn't do it, I still did it. I was determined not to live with the regret and all those what-ifs, simply because I did not try.

What idea do you have for an entrepreneurial endeavor? How would your life be different if you followed your heart rather than the path of least resistance? Who is it you want to help? And most of all, what is the why that drives you? Answer these questions, and be willing to step up to the plate. Don't lie to yourself. Remember that nothing works unless you do! Your life comes with a guarantee; however, you are the guarantor. Live your life free of regret!

LIVING LIFE ON PURPOSE

Arlene Spann

I have come to realize that most of my life, I was preparing to be an entrepreneur through my own #personalaspirations.

I grew up in North Carolina, in the farmlands, and our farm was, indeed, a business. During the harvest months, my parents made us pick cotton to be sold at the gin. We planted, cropped, and sold tobacco to the local warehouse. We picked and sold surplus cucumbers, corn, tomatoes, and fruit and vegetables. My dad was a hunter, and he sold rabbit and deer. As a family, we often went fishing and sold all our surplus catch for a profit.

During the off season, my mother often said, especially during my high school years, "Girl, you always have your head in something at that school." It was true, because being from the small town of Wise, my closest neighbors and peers lived miles away. Even though I had loving siblings, it just wasn't the same as interaction with my peers in the classroom. I was a social, outgoing person and was involved in as many after-school activities as possible.

I was also a problem-solver. I needed to be able to interact with my peers, and the school needed students to participate in band, choir, the library club, and Future Homemakers of America. I saw myself as a solution to the school's problem.

I worked hard to learn the music and felt I was qualified to fill the gaps in band and choir. I also loved to read, so I was happy to assist the librarian with shelving books. Future Homemakers of America needed members, and I definitely qualified as a future homemaker; later in life, I became a teenage mother. You might ask, "What do any of these extracurricular things have to do with being an entrepreneur?" Simple. It's significant, because an entrepreneur mindset begins with recognizing that there are problems in life and that you may very well have or be the solution to those problems.

When I became a teen mother, I needed money for personal and family needs, as well as the expenses of the various high school activities I was involved in. So what did I do? I became a young entrepreneur. I helped my mother sell candy and perfume, and I also subscribed to *Grit Newspaper* and began to sell magazines to students, teachers, distant neighbors, relatives, and friends.

What does being an entrepreneur mean to you? While we may yearn for financial freedom, we live in a world that expects us to finish high school, go to college, get married, find a good job, and retire some forty years later. Then, perhaps, if you are ambitious, you can start a business of your own.

I finished high school in June of 1976. In August of that year, I enrolled at Atlantic Community College in Mays Landing, determined to play the typical American success model out to the letter. A year after I enrolled, I found myself preparing to return to North Carolina to be married to a man I'd met while visiting family in New Jersey two years prior. I wanted to succeed at the society-inflicted success model that was crowding my mind, even though I was repulsed by the idea of working for someone else. That thought was always tugging at the back of my mind.

It was decision-making time. Taking responsibility for getting things done was a driving force for #problemsolving. I was now faced with another pregnancy, as an unwed mother. The American success model began to look dim, and I needed a solution so I quickly became proactive.

Once I knew for certain that I was pregnant, I shared the news with the father-to-be. He simply said he wanted the child to have his name. Rather than shun the situation, I met it head on and hesitantly agreed when he asked me to marry him. While I indeed had my share of problems, I was also a team player who saw it as a chance to have a family of my own. Ultimately, I decided to leave college, get married, and become a mother once more.

In August of 1977, I embarked on a new, complex journey, against my parents' wishes. I would find myself fulfilling another part of the American dream as I stood before the justice of peace in Warrenton, North Carolina, exchanging vows with my very tall groom; I, myself, was only four-eleven to his six-three. Neither of my parents was present, but I had been presented with a challenge, and I thought everything would best be solved by marrying the father of the child I was carrying. It was all part of the sweet makings of an entrepreneur, even if I didn't realize it at the time.

In 1978, in an attempt to refocus and get back on track with the educational part of the American dream, I transferred my college credits from the college in New Jersey to the Vance Granville Community College in Henderson, North Carolina. I had attended that college for almost two semesters when our marriage began to deteriorate. We were a young couple, unsure what to do about our marital problems, but we thought a change of scenery might help. We agreed to uproot from North Carolina and live in Washington DC. I was sure I would be able to fulfill the next item on the to-do list for the American dream in our nation's capital.

After just one week in DC, I ventured out in search of a good government job. Finally, I felt a sense of real accomplishment when, one month later, I landed a position as a personnel clerk for the DC Department of Recreation. Just like that, problem solved!

I was now officially a wage earner, following instructions, clocking in and out, and living on a fixed income. I thought I had arrived, that I was on my way up the government ladder of success. However, the inescapable reality was that everything at home was in turmoil. We had problems, and they led to constant arguments, disagreements, and accusations. Ultimately, my first marriage dissolved and ended in divorce.

Though somewhat confused and dumbfounded about going from wife to single parent again so quickly, I still had my good government job.

Saturday, March 8, 1980 was a day I shall always remember. I arrived at the babysitter to pick up my two children, Angela and Paul. My eyes somewhat seductively caught the gaze of a muscular man who was sitting on the couch, a man I'd never met before. "Hi. My name is Jerome," he said in a mesmerizing accent. Amidst all the background of women's rights debates on television, I heard him laughing as he engaged and interacted kindly with my children. He had such an irresistible way about him, and after he briefly excused himself, he returned wearing a three-piece, burgundy suit.

Still mesmerized, I watched as he walked approximately twelve steps toward the tall, brown exit door that led to the hallway. I continued to stare as he turned and said in that Southern-fried accent of his, "Nice to meet you."

While it was truly none of my business where he was going, I asked him. As if thunderstruck by a strong role reversal of emotions in my heart, emotions I could not explain, my lips blurted out, "I'll take you out." In the back of my mind, I could hear a small voice asking, *What are you doing? You're just getting over one rocky marriage.*

Time stood still for a moment before Jerome turned and asked, his brown eyes meeting mine, "Do you have a car?"

"Yes," I responded, overjoyed that he'd agreed to go out with me.

As I got to know Jerome, I was very impressed with his entrepreneurial work ethic, and I developed a trusting relationship with him. He was a generous, compassionate, confident, hardworking man with an enterprising spirit. I saw him as a man of character, someone who yearned to leave the constraints of working for others and work for himself instead. With my first failed marriage long behind me, I happily exchanged vows with that #enterprisingentrepreneur, Jerome Spann, and are still married today.

While working in my government positions was often exciting and enjoyable, like my husband Jerome and many other entrepreneurs, I wanted to be able to punch my own timecard. I no longer wanted to allow others to hold my career in their hands. My road to entrepreneurship is one of believing in my ability and looking at the possibilities for the future.

Life requires us to perform many duties, and schooling our children is one of them. One enjoyable decision was to home-school my child. My entrepreneurial spirit then enabled me to branch out to become a cooperative home-school. We branched out and partnered with other parents with a small fee for service arrangement. I even hired my children as secretary and teacher's assistant. My reward was watching the children flourish, blossom, and grow. Eventually, my children graduated and went on to college. What a major accomplishment on the road to being an entrepreneur! I built myself up and honed my skills by volunteering and often gravitated toward leadership and teaching positions.

Another of our meaningful duties in life is to visit our doctor yearly. It may not always be exciting or even enjoyable, but it is important. I fulfilled this duty and discovered that I was pre-diabetic, overweight, and had high cholesterol. Prayer came to my aid during that trying time in my life. What had started out as a normal, routine doctor visit became the catalyst for me to go on a quest to rid myself of these newfound ailments. To solve those grim diagnoses and live a more vibrant, healthier life, a new chapter had to be opened in my story. I had to think back to my problem-solving days, to reframe my thinking, to get out of my own way and step out of my comfort zone, to eat healthier and move my body more. I took a risk and went on a journey to make myself healthier.

Through this healthier eating and living, I saw changes. I had to stay focused, and I learned by doing. I rediscovered my entrepreneurial purpose when people began to ask me what I was doing to lose weight, and I wanted to help others become healthier too. God inspired me with a little nudge from my husband Jerome to launch a program called Arlene Spann S.W.E.A.T.S. My new vision was to find strength through my pain. I began to seek self-help programs, training, and personal development seminars, workshops, and conferences. I developed a website, made business cards, and created a logo to let others know I was in business.

Where am I today? I am now an entrepreneur living life on purpose. As the founder, president, and CEO of Arlene Spann S.W.E.A.T.S., I now host my own workshops and seminars. I speak as often as I can, sharing what I know to help others live a healthier lifestyle. I inspire and empower others to take control of every aspect of their lives so they can succeed and reach their highest potential, their God-given purpose. For me, being an entrepreneur is and always really has been a way of life.

FORCED FROM THE NEST

Jae-Mello Spence

*A*h, the nest. If we look at the symbolism of that cozy little place, we can see why it is necessary to be pushed from it. The nest resembles safety and protection, a place where the mother bird hatches her babies for safekeeping. Eventually, though, there comes a time when Mama Bird begins to nudge the babies to go out and fly, so they can learn to find their own food and build their own nests. Sometimes we stay in our nests—our jobs or our bad situations—because they seem so familiar; it's always easier to stay in the familiar. Eventually, though, we outgrow the nest, and we will be forced out due to lack of room; no longer will that cozy little nest be comfortable. We must fly out to gain more, to experience more, and to do what we are purposed to do. We must be evicted from the nest! God has a way of shaking the nest and making it uncomfortable so we must get out.

Having been through so much in life, I'd love to share how I've overcome. I still have much growing to do, but I know I am finally on the right path. My name is Jae Spence. I was born to a single mother in Harlem, New York. I grew up in a family where dream-chasing was a rare commodity. Although I was gifted with many talents, my mother and seven aunts and uncles weren't all dream-chasers. Fear kept my mother from fulfilling her dreams, and it seemed to lurk all around me. My dad was not involved in my life during my childhood, and I was his secret for the better part of my life, another symptom of fear. I remember the good times, all those family gatherings. My family seemed to find me funny and enjoyed having me around. I remember them asking me to act or to imitate some character, and it was in those simple, laughable moments that I learned just how much joy acting and singing could bring. Little did I know then that it would be my way to freedom!

Trauma

I had my share of challenges. I was molested as a child, and in my teenage years, I witnessed the abuse of my mother. I had my first child at seventeen and my second at eighteen. I was a mother of two at eighteen, and I had no idea how to care to my kids; I only knew I had to figure it out. At twenty, I married a minister who abused me, a secret I carried for years because I was too ashamed to tell anyone. *Who would even believe me?* I wondered. I had my third child during that marriage.

One day, I'd had enough, so I moved myself and my children into a one-bedroom apartment. I had nothing but the Lord, and I was sure He would see me through.

I made it through those difficult times and met another man, who was great to me and my children, a welcomed distraction to my abused past. We weren't married long before he died prematurely. I was pregnant with my fourth child, and his death really took a toll on me. I didn't understand why he had died; he was so young and healthy. To make matters worse, I checked my bank account one day to find that all my money was gone. It was then that I discovered that the autopsy had found excessive cocaine and alcohol in his system, a problem I wasn't even aware he had. Needless to say, I was broken and destroyed. I worried, *what am I gonna do now, with this big belly, no money, and no job*? It was especially difficult because I was unable to work due to pregnancy complications. Again, God looked out for us.

I moved to Rhode Island to start my life anew. It was a tough road, and nothing was ever easy, but I was seemingly making progress. Then, in 2003, I received a call to let me know that my younger brother, a brother I was very close to, had shot himself in the head. I can't even tell you the devastation I felt. My life seemed to be put on hold, and I wasn't sure if I even wanted to go on. Fortunately, I survived.

I eventually married again, and when I did, I experienced abuse on a whole different level. The deception and emotional abuse was even harder on me than the physical abuse I'd experienced before. My fifth child came from that tumultuous union,

I can only say that at that time in my life, Dysfunction might as well have been my middle name. I now realize the repeated turmoil was all because I hadn't dealt with the first issue. I wasn't raised to face my challenges or experience pain. On the contrary, I knew that strong women could handle abuse and get over it. Since I wanted to be perceived that way, I dared not tell anyone or get help from a therapist, a sure sign of weakness. Some abused women rely on drugs, alcohol, or smoking as an escape, but I chose love as mine. I was addicted to love and began searching for it in all the wrong places, until allowed my true and first love, love Himself, to show me the right way—an un-perverted love I had never seen or experienced before.

In the face of such tragedies, many would have sure reason to give up, lose their mind, or even lose their spirit. For me, the fight was on. I trusted God and knew He would not allow the enemy to in. I knew all along that He had called me to greater things than the traumas I'd suffered.

The Fight

Determined not to give up, I went back to school and earned my associate's degree. Several years later, I went back to get my bachelor's. In the interim, I started my own business. Although I had every reason to give up, I couldn't. I absolutely wouldn't. Instead of using my circumstances as a crutch, I considered them a force to push me out of the nest of safety, into the promise of God. His promise for me is to win and to prosper, and to this day, I stand on that.

I have been singing and acting as long as I can remember, and I may have inherited some of it from my mother, who has a beautiful voice. I have been in theater and recorded in studios with groups and for some well-known artists. I have been in ministry, sung in churches, and traveled to preach and sing for years.

I still remember the day the business idea came to mind. A young lady approached me to ask if I could teach her how to sing. I had never thought of doing such a thing and couldn't even imagine how I would do it, yet it sparked the intention. It was many years after that conversation before the idea came to fruition, but it did happen. I was finally going to be doing something I loved and found my passion, a gift from God. I had been signing and being a blessing to others, and now I could use that blessing to create and offer freedom and so much more.

The Moments that Changed Me

I recall my first time handing out business cards and bravely signing up to host my very first class for the town of North Kingstown. I was so insecure and unprepared, and I felt vulnerable and incapable, with very little confidence. I knew I could sing, but teaching doesn't come naturally or easily.

The date of my first Saturday class arrived, and five students had paid to take it. I was terrified, but I really didn't have to be. After all, God certainly has a way of divinely orchestrating things.

This first class was a test, of sorts, and I was completely insecure, even when the students told me they enjoyed and learned from it. I knew I had so much more to offer. One of those first students, Clarissa Walker, eventually became a best friend and she also just so happened to have a great business head on her shoulders, as she was quite an entrepreneur herself. She helped me build my business, gave me marketing ideas, and blessed me in ways I can't even begin to name. From our friendship came new business cards, a business plan, a new name, a "doing business as…" (DBA) in my state, and an efficient way to run my small business. God is so good! I am reminded of a song called "Trust in the Lord." The lyrics are, "Troubles come, but they won't last. Deep in my heart, I trust…"

Inspiration

Inspiration can come from anything, and I can say Lenny, my little brother, was an inspiration for me. He was a young, handsome, gifted young man who always reminded me that I should aspire to more. "We need to start a business. You need to sing," he often said. Even his untimely death inspired me, forcing me to realize that I would never be fulfilled in life without following my dreams and doing what I am called to do.

Why a business though?

The funny thing is, I spent years trying to find what I thought I wanted to do. I remember going to school to be a forensic psychologist, then later striving toward being a teacher's assistant, then a legal assistant, then earning my BS in human services—all of which are great accomplishments. I have worked as an office manager, a billing representative, a legal assistant, and a teacher's assistant, but none of these jobs fulfilled my desire, which I now know is to create. One of the problems with a regular job is that there are limits placed on your creativity. This doesn't mean the people I worked for didn't agree with my creativity; in many cases, they did, but it just didn't always fit into their plan. The trouble was that their plan was not my plan.

The nest signifies safety, and that was what a traditional job represented for me. It was a safe way to survive, a safety net, but it inhibited my dreams. I always felt restless at work, as if it wasn't enough for me and I needed something more. I never enjoyed being the lead for someone else's dream. *What about mine?* my head screamed every minute while I was on someone else's clock.

The dream took shape in 2008 and has grown from doing town run programs to actually having private students. I have directed the NK Drama Group of over seventy-five young people. I have also run vocal camps and created after-school vocal programs, all the while taking my private students to the next level!

Freedom

I am elated to have lost my J.O.B. I am now free to create, to evolve, and to make a difference the way I was called to do. Acting and singing had always been an escape for me, but hearing my students say that working with me has built their confidence and brought them healing and peace now drives me.

I have the room to teach and to learn as well. I remember when I first began teaching, one of my students had cochlear implants, which means she'd been deaf for most of her life. I helped that student, and we learned together what worked and didn't work for her. That experience took me to another level in vocal training.

I also had a student who didn't necessarily wish to sing. Instead, she wanted to learn to speak clearly, as she was involved with radio broadcasting. With the same breathing techniques I taught singers, I was able to help her gain a better grasp on her speaking, making it easier for her to engage her listeners and get her point clearly across.

Expression of any kind offers healing, and movement and singing have many benefits of their own. There is an inspirational story of U.S. Representative Gabriel Gifford, who was tragically shot in the head by a troubled man back in 2011. In an article I read, it was written that a woman came in and played Mrs. Gifford's favorite song, "This Little Light of Mine." At a time when she could hardly speak, she could still sing along to that happy little tune. She couldn't remember much of the lyrics, but she recalled the melody, the sound of music, and it helped her find healing and recovery. She was shot in the left side of the brain, limiting her speech, but since music is prevalent on both sides of the brain, she was able to train the healthy right side to speak again.

Music has been healing, and being able to write my feelings and express them in song has done wonders for my sanity during some very hard times. I am inclined to share a particular post from a student. She was feeling depressed, sometimes even suicidal because of some things that were going on in her life. I had often encouraged her with my words, but it was the music she mentioned in this post of thanks. She said she thought back on a song she had learned with me, and that song helped her through her challenges. She was rediscovering the power in singing, movement, and music.

That is why I do what I do, to encourage, inspire, and help people find healing through expression. My freedom is in this expression as well. I encourage you, whether you want to be a professional singer or not, to try a vocal/movement class. It's more than just singing. I also teach, diction, coincidence, stage presence, mic control, movement, and emoting, and it's a great release. My business name is Melodious Vocals, and our motto is, "We take your voice to the next level." I would love to work with you help you learn the greatness of expression in speaking, song, movement, emoting, and writing. I host private or group lessons and have created vocal programs for seniors who just want to sing for fun to preschoolers who want to jump and dance. I've helped people prepare for big auditions, such as for *The Voice* and *American Idol*, and I have coached for poetry slams. Music, movement, and song have limitless possibilities and can be life changing in the best way! Contact Jae Spence at 401-219-6800. Skype and Ovoo lessons are available if you are out of state.

KNOW YOUR WORTH

*H*ave you ever gone to a restaurant where a certain dish cost an exuberant amount of money? Maybe you've gone shopping and have done a double-take on the price tag, because you were sure you'd looked at it wrong. Perhaps it's a bit shocking to you, as a consumer, but the truth is, these prices are set that way because the businesses know their worth and are simply not afraid to show it.

You must learn and know your worth and not to be afraid to ask for the dollar amount that matches your expertise. This is often a difficult concept for novice entrepreneurs to grasp; it's hard to believe anyone would pay for your services, your voice, your food, your time, or your thoughts, but they will, as long as you strive to genuinely under promise and over deliver. A good friend of mine, Che Brown, once said, "Once you learn how to ask with confidence, the rest will fall into place. If you have a product or service that answers the problem someone has, they have no choice but to honor your price." It makes a lot of sense if you think about it!

Keep in mind that once you put that price out there, you have got to produce. You cannot ask for top dollar and rollout mediocre results. Not only will you lose a customer; but you will also lose your reputation. It is better to start out modestly, being fair to yourself and the customer. When you become a revered expert in your field, you can ask for top dollar, and you'll get it! Why? Because you know and confidently demonstrate your worth.

Soon, you will gain a market that is faithful to you, and you will anticipate new products or services to patronize and refer to friends, colleagues, and loved ones. That is the magic of entrepreneurship, it starts with one happy customer getting all you promised them, and before you know it, your phone is ringing off the hook.

On the flipside, if you've made mistakes—as many of us have—it is best to rebrand, reinvent, and recompense the situation. Make it right and make it right fast. Don't let it linger. Do what you can to make that disgruntled customer happy and to avoid that pitfall again. You are going to make mistakes, some bigger than others, but the true growth and test is whether or not you learn and grow from it. Accountability will also build your worth, because you will be known as an action-taker opposed to an excuse-maker.

MORE TEARS THAN FEARS

Shavon Goodwin

I remember the day I walked out on corporate America because I was not able to leave to pick up my sick daughter from daycare when she had a temperature of 104. When my manager asked what I was going to do, my reply was, "I don't know what you're going to do, but I know what I'm going to do." I did just that: I walked out.

In fact, I had already started taking classes at night at a local community college for cosmetology. Within six years, I discovered that the nine-to-five was just not for me. I did want to work on other people's terms. As a single mom, I only wanted to work for myself, so I decided to do pursue cosmetology. I was great at it, but I eventually realized it was more of a way out than a dream. Even though it wasn't my heart's desire, I felt it would be one way to have my own business. A year later, I graduated. Pregnant with my fourth daughter, I walked across the stage to receive my diploma, and then I went out to start my venture into the world of hair.

I was a twenty-seven-year-old beautician. The gas prices has skyrocketed and everyone was in a complete panic, desperately trying to figure out how to cut back and survive. One of the things they cut back on was getting their hair done. I was sometimes paid with rolls of coins, and some clients even asked how they could do what I did and do their own hair at home, because they could not afford to keep coming to me.

I was single mother of four daughters, and I fell into a deep depression. In a time of despair, when the economy went haywire, I didn't have enough love for my business to fight for it. I felt empty and void, like my prayers were not being answered. I didn't even want to get out of bed. It was as if I'd just had given up. I was lost, consumed by pain. I was tired of being broke, tired of trying to figure out how I was going to survive, how I was going to beat poverty.

Then one day I just snapped out of it. I bounced back somehow, and I know it was by the grace of God. He had planted a drive, an urge in me. I went from not wanting to crawl out of bed to searching for something better. I knew there had to be something out there. *What am I supposed to do?* I questioned myself.

I started doing some research and thought about my life. I tried to understand why some of the people I'd graduated with were doing so well, yet my amazing talents had gotten me nowhere. I was just suffering. As I evaluated that, I started to recognize that none of my successful former classmates lived in my town anymore; they had all relocated. It was then that I knew what I had to do. I didn't know where to go, but I had to go somewhere.

I had always love fashion, and that had been my dream, but when I became a teenage mom at sixteen, I had to give up those dreams and settle for a regular nine-to-five. I decided to research various colleges to see who offered fashion design. In the meantime, I had to do my remaining clients' hair at home, because I couldn't afford to pay booth rent at the salon anymore.

One day, seemingly out of the blue, I received a phone call from an unknown number. I never answer numbers I don't recognize, but for some reason, I answered it that day. It was a lady by the name of Crystal, an administrator at the Art Institute of Atlanta. She quickly persuaded me to visit the school; even though I was in the midst of turmoil, trying to figure out what I was going to do and how I was going to survive, I worked out a way to meet with her.

Crystal had the most amazing personality. With a great deal of joy and enthusiasm, she showed me around the school, and I fell in love with the place. She then asked, "Do what you want to go ahead and register and start in August?"

I hesitated. I had no idea how I was going to relocate in time to start school on August 7, my birthday, but Crystal would not back down. She urged me to start in August, and I ultimately decided that I would. I had no idea how it would work out, but I knew I was going to soon find out.

I found an affordable, roomy enough house in Marietta for me and my children. When I finally broke the news to my clients, friends, and some family, the reaction was not all good. Everyone thought I was crazy to uproot my kids and move away with no support or help. Many thought I was running from something, and they were right; I was running from complacency, running to fulfill my dreams.

On August 7, the first day of school, I stepped out of my truck and stood in the parking lot, full of joy and gratitude. I took a deep breath and took it all in. In every class, I sat right in the front row. I wanted to make sure I did not miss a thing, because I was so grateful to have a second chance at my dream.

It was not all rosy though. In fact, 80 percent of the time, I prayed that I would make it to school and home again; I often feared I might run out of gas. Somehow, I always made it through. Sometimes, someone would call and ask if I needed anything, or, strangely, I would find just enough money in my bank account. I knew God had not carried me so far just to desert me, so I just continued to step out in faith and go to school, get the best grades I could, and strive for perfect attendance. I knew if I kept my GPA up, I could get grants, and those would help because I still had some out-of-pocket to pay that wasn't covered by my Pell grant. If I maintained perfect attendance, I received $100 at the end of the quarter, and that sounded good to me. I needed any extra money I could get, because I was really struggling to pay the bills.

I always went the extra mile on my schoolwork because I had to make good grades; I had a lot to lose if I didn't. Because of that, I had a hard time making friends; many people thought I was a goody two-shoes, trying to make everyone else look bad. What they didn't know was that I was keeping my twelve-year-old daughter up at night so she could hold the flashlight for me. I often finished my work in the dark, because we had no electricity for a little over a month. We charged my cell phone in the apartment complex laundry room, and I had to re-pack the freezer with new ice every day to keep what little food we had from spoiling. My kids had to hurry and finish their homework after school, before we lost daylight. To iron our clothes, I put water in the iron and heated it on the gas stove. We had plenty of flashlights, so I made sure to read to my children every night. Every morning, I woke up and thanked God that I had gas, so I was able to bath in hot water, cook, and iron. My classmates judged me without really understanding what I was dealing with, because I was always happy. I refused to let my obstacles block my vision. I could not allow myself to lose focus.

Fortunately, I was able to get our electric turned on right before it started to get cold. My kids were excited; they had said all they wanted for Christmas was lights, and on December 14, 2010, I intended to give them just that. We excitedly cleaned the apartment and put up a Christmas tree, though we had no lights to put on it yet. I decided to take out the trash and check the mail, and I drove down to do it because we lived in a large complex. As I thumbed through the mail, glancing at all those bills, I wondered how in the world I would be able to get my kids anything for Christmas, as I was already immersed in a grave finan-cial struggle. At that very moment, something came over me. I simply froze. All I could do was praise God. "Thank you, Jesus," I repeated over and over, consumed by gratitude, with tears running down my cheeks.

Once I came to my senses and regained my mobility, I returned to my apartment. Several people were running around, and I wondered what in the world was going on. I glanced up at my apartment and saw smoke pouring from it. *What have those kids done?* I thought in horror. I imagined they had put something in the microwave for too long and cracked the door to let the smoke out. When I hurried to my apartment, I saw enormous, orange flames and black smoke covering my door. I frantically looked around but saw no signs of my children. "My kids!" I said, breathless, when a man grabbed me away.

"They're out," he said. "They're standing by my apartment."

Great relief washed over me once I knew they were safe, and I rushed over to check on them.

The outcome of the fire was not good at all. I had lost everything—every single thing—other than my kids and my portfolio. *God is amazing,* I thought. I had finals the next day, and I had worked my butt off. My portfolio had been in the kitchen, where the fire started, and it was the only remotely recognizable item left in that smoldering room; everything else had been completely destroyed.

We stayed in a hotel that night. Red Cross covered the bill for three days. I went from not knowing how I was going to pay my bills, how I was going to give my children any semblance of Christmas, to about $6,000 in days, money from people I did not even know. People who knew me or my mother just so happened to know people who wanted to help. I did not even have to use any of those kind donations for Christmas gifts, because my daughter's reading tutor's was a wealthy lawyer, and they replaced just about everything we lost.

I eventually found another place to stay, a house this time, in a great part of town, with a great school system. I did not attend school that next semester, because I had so much going on. I was sick, and I attributed it to being stressed out, but as it turned out, I was actually pregnant with my fifth child.

I returned to school that spring quarter, and I was excited to get back in the flow of things. I was afraid of running out of money, and I wanted to be able to pay my bills, so I did not buy any books. I had a great plan, or so I thought, until I was advised by one of my teachers that I had a hold and could not attend class until that was taken care of. I thought it was some kind of mistake, so I hurried to get the issue resolved, because I hated missing even class. At the Student Services Office, I stood in the long line and waited. I was advised that I had to make a payment of $675 to be able to attend classes that semester, and they put me on a payment plan for the rest. Having no other choice, I made the payment and arrangements. I would deal with everything else as it came to me, and I would continue with my semester with faith and gratitude, as usual.

I noticed that we never used our books outside of class for my fashion design class. For my painting class, I checked out a library book similar to the class book. We had chapter tests once every two weeks, so I made copies of all the pages from a classmate's book. When I had no money for copies, I borrowed the book from a guy who sat next to me; all weekend before the test, I just sat and copied the chapters by hand.

One day in my fashion design class, my teacher wanted each of us to stand up and tell the class about ourselves. When it was my turn, I told them all about me and my children. "I'm a single mom of four daughters," I said, "and I am pregnant with my fifth."

My honesty seemed to irritate the teacher, and she wanted to make a mockery of me. "You need to go home and take care of your kids," she said. Then she turned to the other, younger students in the class and said, "Girls, don't ever have that many kids without being married, because no one will ever want you. Your vagina will have no more elasticity."

From that day forward, the teacher had it in for me. What she didn't know was that I was used to being insulted, and I really didn't care. A day came, though, when she did get to me.

We were told to make a fashion vision board. When I do something, I always try to go above and beyond. Besides the fact that I had a real passion for what I was studying, I also needed to make the best grades as possible. To present the best possible project, I spent money I had intended to put toward a bill, but I had to give it my all.

I was so proud of my fashion vision board. It was nice, and I had put a lot of thought into it and made sure it included everything the teacher had asked for. I was a little late to her class that day and arrived at 8:08 a.m. I quietly walked in and placed my vision board down behind everyone else's.

When the teacher got to my project, she lifted it up and showed the other students, many of whom gasped with quiet amazement. "This is garbage," the teacher said. "This is F work. It's not even on foam board. This is absolute trash." Then she dropped my board carelessly on the floor. I still remember the sound it made when it met the tile.

I was furious, but I somehow managed to remain composed for the duration of the class. After class was dismissed, I politely went up to her and advised her that when I asked for foam board at Michael's, that was what they had given me. I also explained that I had never used foam board before, so I had no idea it was the wrong thing. Of course she had no problem letting me know that she did not care, and I left the classroom as mad as I was hurt. I had worked hard for that grade, investing my time, thought, and money, only to receive an undeserved F.

I sat in my truck and cried and cried that day. I had no desire to go to my other class, so I drove home. The next day, I was mad as hell at myself. I had allowed that teacher to get the best of me, and in the process, I had blown my chances at perfect attendance. I made a vow to myself that day that I would never again allow anyone to control me so that I would lose sight of my goals, and I planned to redeem my grade by any means necessary.

Our final project was worth a great percentage of our final grade, and she sprung it on us at the last minute. We were instructed to create a portfolio of twenty outfits we had designed, based off of our vision board. At eight months pregnant, I stayed up all night, drawing, coloring, and putting my portfolio together. When daylight came, I still wasn't finished; two of my daughters helped be color a sketch before they rushed out of the house to catch their bus. I had no time to take a bath, knowing that if I was late to class on time, she would not accept my project. My feet were swollen from sitting up at the kitchen table all night, but I got into my car and headed to school. I was really still not finished, as one of my sketches still needed to be colored. My mind said, Good job. *You did your best,* but my will said, *Color and drive. You can't walk into her class half-stepping.* I was finally able to complete everything. I walked into the classroom tired and possibly stinking, but in the end, I was proud of myself.

The teacher walked by and looked through my portfolio, then said to me, "Oh, you completed it? You finished? I was not expecting you to. No one in any of my classes has ever finished." She then added, "I must say that you amaze me. I don't know how you managed, with four kids and a pregnancy. I admire you."

Ultimately, in spite of the many challenges and my battles with that difficult teacher, I made all A's that semester and ended up on the dean's list with a 4.0 GPA.

I was not able to go back to school the following fall semester. The Obama childcare had run out of funds, and I was in no financial state to be able to afford online classes, now that they were double the tuition I was already struggling to keep up with. I coasted for the next two years, just trying to make ends meet. I started making custom tutu outfits for little girls. I even put on a fashion show, designing outfits for my daughters, my makeshift models, to wear, but I didn't make any profits or gains from that.

I was a new mother again, of a sixth daughter, and I had fallen into a depression, I only pulled myself out of bed when I had to care for my children. Then I was introduced to a network marketing company for Organo Gold, a healthy coffee. I was not a coffee-drinker, so I did not really get the big rah-rah over it, but someone I cared about invited me to a meeting to check it out, so I went. The people I met there claimed they'd made millions with the company, so I tried the product. As I thought about the meeting and what I'd learned there, it started to make sense, but what really activated me to take part in the company was the way the coffee made me feel. I was rejuvenated, not depressed anymore.

Every Sunday and Wednesday night, the company and/ or my team would had group calls, from which I gleaned a great deal of information. I heard about many wonderful books and began reading more and more. Eventually, my mindset began to change, and I started looking at everything in life from a different perspective.

One thing we were taught in training was that when we had our Jazz Mixers, get-togethers to introduce people to the coffee products, we should always tell our story about why we had decided to start our own Organo Gold coffee distributor business. The weirdest thing happened: I started talking to people.

I had never been much of a people person, especially when it came to strangers, but every time I hosted a Jazz Mixer, several women attended. Soon, I noticed that something great was happening. The women began to open up, allowing themselves to be vulnerable. They talked about the things they'd been through, and we all really bonded with one another. I was soon full of joy, because I knew something greater was taking place.

At one of the Jazz Mixers, I was actually struggling to hold back my tears as I muttered, "Okay, God. Use me." That is exactly what He has been doing ever since, because I am now a motional speaker for women and teenage girls.

In time, a children's book came to me, and I am in the process of publishing it. *A Princess in Me* was created by unlocking and clearing out my bondage, the result of meeting and observing girls with absent or unworthy fathers in their lives.

No, I did not become a millionaire like some of the others in the network marketing company, but I can only assume it was not meant for me to have millions, at least not yet. I realized that when I opened a business checking account with nothing in my hand. I have a story, a voice that allows others to see that you can do it with nothing in your hand. All you have to do is decide that you and your dreams *are* worth fighting for, that you must do what it takes to acquire your purpose. Have faith! Belief will open the mind, even when things look unattainable to the natural eye. Don't become discouraged when your plan seeps out of your hand like sand, because everything happens how it is supposed to.

If I hadn't gone to school, I never would have discovered how creative I am, I never would have known that I have drawing and painting skills. I never would have found out how strong my will to succeed and persevere really is. If I wouldn't have gotten into network marketing,

I wouldn't have started speaking to people, really bonding with them. Now I speak to everyone I meet, wearing a bright smile on my face, embodied with joy, because I have peace and because I'm walking in my purpose.

Boy, were my plans very different, but I wouldn't change a thing, because it all formed the foundation for my path to my purpose!

THE PARADIGM SHIFT

Barrett Mathews

*J*ust like everyone else in my generation who grew up in the Washington DC suburbs, I was expected to go to school to get a good education, to earn good grades that would allow me to enroll in college, to graduate from college and get a—wait for it—good job!

We all heard that same refrain in the neighborhood where I lived, and why not? My parents were middle-class, working folks, with so-called good government jobs. We lived less than ten minutes from the DC line, in Glenarden, Maryland, and government jobs were thought to mean security for decades to come. For African American families, whose parents and grandparents had grown up in poverty, such an opportunity was often thought of as the path to the American dream. My parents were born during the Great Depression, in large families, so they knew the value of hard work and appreciated their steady, bi-weekly paychecks. Both of them worked for over thirty years as U.S. government employees, and they taught their four children to follow in their footsteps, with an emphasis on education and always doing our best.

As for me, my mindset was always a little different; I'd never been much of a follower. Although I appreciated all that my parents did to make my life as seamless as possible throughout my childhood, I never saw myself working for the government. It just wasn't for me. I never saw myself commuting daily, watching the clock, and working in the confines of a cubicle. I'm not saying people shouldn't do it, but it was not for me, and I knew that even as a child.

I remember the days of my youth, when I earned income by cutting the neighbor's grass. At the time, it didn't seem like a signature moment, but as I look back, I can see that it was very important to my mindset, and it created a shift in my thinking. A guy who later became a good friend and football teammate of mine delivered newspapers in our neighborhood early in the morning. His name was Joe Devane, and he went on to start a business while he was in college. He had a strong work ethic and a developing entrepreneurial mindset early on in life, and that mindset carried him to where he is now. As I think back, I had a certain admiration for what he did as a young man. I also wish I had thought outside of my box and created a lawn-cutting service, employing the other neighborhood kids. Hindsight certainly is twenty/twenty.

But being a business owner was not something that was encouraged or taught to me as a child. Rather, the focus was on working and studying hard, and that was what we did. Business ownership was not taught in school either, nor were there many entrepreneurial examples in my life, outside my daily circle. Nevertheless, there was always something that drove me away from the norm. I had a desire to have my own money. I knew my parents worked extremely hard to give their children the best life they could. We never wanted for anything; in retrospect, I admit we were probably spoiled by some assertions, though we were always appreciative of what we had and the love we received. Because of the appreciation of my parents' work, I wanted to work for my own spending money. So, at the ripe old age of thirteen, I got a summer job, thanks to my cousin, who was instrumental in the community government.

The job was hard work. I had to cut and trim the tall grass and weeds around the community, and my only supplies and tools were my jeans, my boots, and my sickle. I sweated heavily every day, but it was an honest paycheck and helped to instill in me a strong work ethic— so much so that as a teenager, I wanted a summer job every year. It afforded me the chance to buy a drum set, something I desperately wanted, and I joined my school band. Seeing the rewards of your hard work is an immeasurable experience for a young person. It can catapult you into creating and achieving goals from that point on.

In high school, I had the opportunity to work in a program called Youth Conservation Corps (YCC). It was a Department of Agriculture (DOA) initiative to help high-schoolers gain work experience while beautifying the land owned by the DOA. The work was very similar to that of my first summer job, except that we did much more than cut and trim grass. We also worked on farms, cleaning up after animals, and we learned to not only tear away, but also to build up the community surrounding the government facilities. Most of all, I was able to forge relationships and friendships. This asset proved very valuable in my future as an entrepreneur. My work experience progressed, and after my second year with the YCC, I was a youth leader. There, I learned the fine art of delegation.

Next, I moved on to work in the construction field. At only seventeen, I was not legally supposed to work there, but my football coach was able to pull a few strings with his friends. It was, by far, the hardest work I'd ever done. Construction definitely tested my mettle and taught me that I would much rather use my mind and education, something that had been instilled in me by my parents.

Looking back, I realize it was quite a pivotal time for me. As I prepared for college, I was determined not to use my body as a tool; I wanted to use my intellect. Each job I took from that point on—during spring break, Christmas, or summers—was one that allowed me to think and create with my mind. I was able to see the free thinker inside myself and the leader within, of only on a small scale.

I graduated from Hampton University with a bachelor's in mass media arts. At that time, entrepreneurship was not taught among the college curriculum, but I think it would have helped us all. I focused my studies on the areas of television and radio, and I also wrote for the school paper. That was where my leadership and talents began to grow and develop. I excelled as a media personality on campus and even had my own spot as the sportscaster on the school television news program, where I was allowed to write my own copy. I hosted a post-game TV show for the football team and outright defied naysayers who said I couldn't do it. Before long, I was the number-one play-by-play radio announcer for the Hampton football and basketball games. I was named sports producer for the radio station and given the budgeting responsibility for road trips for the announcing team. These responsibilities and opportunities taught me how to be a leader and how to work with deadlines, important attributes for any entrepreneur.

Even with all those qualities developing and coming to fruition within me, I still had the mindset of an employee. Why? Because it was what I had been taught and raised to be. When I graduated college, I was elated to have my honors degree; it was a goal I had met. Still, I knew I had to get a job. It was not easy to get a foot in the door at TV stations, and radio stations were even harder. Eventually, out of sheer desperation and the urging of my parents, I applied for a government job.

Fortunately, I had done several internships, and my last one landed me my first job as assistant director at WUSA-TV in DC. It may sound like some important, grand title, but I was really nothing more than a floor director, telling the talent which camera was pointed at them. I started at a meager annual salary of $13,000 and earned $15,000 in my second year. Then came the signature moment in my life.

I was offered a rare opportunity to move to New York City and work for CBS sports, a major network, just as I had told many of my college classmates I would someday do. Never had I imagined that I would reach that goal by the age of twenty-four, but I did it. I was there for the 1989 football season, working in the Research Department. There, I learned what corporate America is really about. During that eye-opening period, I learned about nepotism, racism, sexism, and all sorts of other –isms I didn't even know existed. I eventually realized I'd been brought in not on my merit, but instead as a token black person to fill a quota, only for my contract not to be renewed after the first season. It was the same for the other African American they'd brought in at the same time and it was all very traumatic and shocking for me. I had never been fired before, but it brought to mind the words of one of my college professors: "You have not worked in television until you have been fired." In my mind, I had earned my stripes in television.

With my trust wavered, I began my search for work in the field of television as an employee for another company. I interviewed with ESPN, BET, and other companies. Most didn't want to hire me because they said I had too much experience for my three years in the workforce. Working for the top news station in DC and the top sports network in the world in 1989-90 made me seem overqualified, even though I really had a lot to learn. The only company that would hire me was a community television station on cable access. I was humbled, but it finally began to open my mind.

It was a postcard that began my paradigm shift. The card was from a lady named Peggy Gist, who worked with Primerica. I met her for an interview, and she asked me about my dreams. She told me what she saw for me and said she could help me achieve those dreams, all while being my own boss. It was new and foreign to me that someone would talk to me in that manner, but it also excited me. It propelled me, and I was ready to go, and in no time at all, I became a financial services professional.

Peggy's coaching helped to develop me into a businessman and an entrepreneur, and it boosted my leadership skills. Most of all, though, she helped to develop my attitude and mindset. I became a tough leader, someone who wanted to win all the time. I'd always had a work ethic, a competitive spirit, and a desire to win, but now I was able to use my intellect and my skills as a mass communicator to teach and lead others, all on my time and my schedule. Peggy truly changed my life. I went on to move to Atlanta, where I opened my own offices with Primerica. The entrepreneurial bug had taken over.

After ten years with the company, though, I was forced to learn a valuable lesson. I mismanaged some of my business and was driven to leave the company at no fault of Primerica. I still had the entrepreneurial bug, though, and it led me to become a real estate appraiser. I was able to still help people, keep my own schedule, and be my own boss. I realized that may people envied my situation, but few had the discipline to work on their own. Many cannot be self-employed because they would make lousy employees for themselves. The entrepreneurial mindset is not for everyone, but it was surely for me.

Around 2007, the mortgage industry hit the wall, and my appraisal work came to an abrupt halt. Still driven by my entrepreneur mindset, I was forced to take a job until I could find my next venture. I was relegated to take a part-time job at Delta Airlines in crew accommodations. It drove me crazy, to the point where I decided to move back to Maryland to become the director of canvassing at Long Fence and Home, a home improvement company. I was still an independent contractor, which gave me the freedom I desired. After a year, the economy forced Long to close my department and several others.

At that point, I was introduced to a business few people knew about, the field of public adjusting. Public adjusters assist home and business owners with property damage claims, ensuring that they are paid fairly and properly by their insurers. I became a state-licensed public adjuster with Metro Public Adjuster, a direct-sales company with a network marketing pay structure. This allowed me to be my own boss, build a team of professionals under me, and generate passive income. I saw the big picture immediately and learned not to make the mistakes I had made with Primerica. I learned to be a success as a public adjuster and a businessman, and my vision began to expand.

While maintaining a successful public adjusting business in different states, I was encouraged by my marketing coach, Trevor Otts, to take my no-nonsense leadership style into the coaching realm, to empower and educate aspiring entrepreneurs. After writing my first book, *Why Didn't You Get It Done? A Guide to Helping You Get off Your Assets*, I began to forge a coaching platform in my company, E2E Systems. E2E helps people move from working for a living to living their dreams. Our goal is to get people to move from employee to entrepreneur. I have been able to travel and speak, empowering and encouraging people the way God intended. Now, with several others, I have more businesses and ventures in the works.

Even as a child, I knew I wasn't a follower. I always felt I was destined to be different and to be great. God made me different, and it was up to me to walk in my purpose. God surrounds us with people to guide us. It is up to us to trust Him and see His guidance in order to see our purpose. My family helped to instill intelligence and a work ethic in me, and life gave me the trials that led to my paradigm shift. If you want to move into entrepreneurship from being and employee, you *must* have a paradigm shift. Do it now, because your purpose walk may be given to someone if you are not willing to take the first step.

TWO WEEKS' NOTICE

Sharlene R. Prince, The Royalty Mindset Coach

*F*ear is not an option when you are aiming high and following your goals and dreams, its presence is lurking and waiting to take hold of your mind, body and spirit, but your burning desires are in charge this time. Taking the plunge and believing in yourself can cause anxiety and confusion, but you know, deep down inside, that you are doing the right thing. How do you know? Well, you know by that burning inferno in middle of your belly that never ceases; no matter what you do, it cannot be satisfied.

I always wanted to own my own business, but the mere thought of branching out on my own was always encumbered by a fear factor. Fear was a deterrent that kept me from taking that next step. I never thought I could really leave the comfort of a stable job that provided my family and me with the security we needed not only to live, but also to survive. My parents raised me with a particular belief system: do well in school, go to college, and then get a good job in my chosen profession. The mindset was always that a good job would give me loyalty, stability, and a foundation on which to build a stable, sound life. Now, we all know job security is no longer a guarantee nowadays, though there are some exceptions.

I have worked on Wall Street, for banks, and for major corporations, but there was always a void and a lack of satisfaction. I always felt smarter than some of my immediate bosses and supervisors, but I knew it would cause issues if I aimed too high, so I had to stay in my lane and wait for the opportunity for a growth spurt to come around. Until an employer offered me a promotion to supervisor, I had never realized how much animosity and tension would go along with it. The very same people who'd claimed to be my friends turned on me, because I was now their boss, placing productivity expectations on them. The connections I'd had quickly deteriorated because I wanted to rise in the company, and it really hurt when they decided to go out for lunch without me; they shared that I was no longer one of them because I had joined the enemies. One of things you have to be aware of is that with growth, especially in business, you will go through cutthroat experiences, jealousy, doubt, and lack of support, and the list continues. However, if you stay strong and steadfast in your beliefs and aim for your goals, blessings will follow. For the first time in my life, I truly understood the transaction of growth in the business industry and what aiming higher truly meant.

We must comprehend that not everyone wants to be a boss and in charge, but I was an exception to that rule. I wanted more out of my life, and the sole path of working for others was not a long-term goal or career choice on my map to success. I was working for a hospital in the evenings and looking through ads daily to find something that would make me feel more satisfied, something that would open the doors of growth. I just couldn't take the lack of respect, and the heavy workload continued to cause dissatisfaction in my life. I began to seek other outlets in an effort to change my life, things that would put me in control of my path and my destiny.

I eventually found a career path that would change my life forever, a career in which I could help people manifest their dreams into reality. After I became a loan officer, nothing was ever the same again. I began working nights at the hospital. After I got off in the mornings and got my kids off to school, I would then rush into the shower and head out to my commission position, which I had to be to by nine a.m. I witnessed people paving the way to their future, making money while helping others obtain their own American dream of homeownership.

Please don't get me wrong: Working in the medical field was very satisfying at times and often produced great rewards. I helped people through very trying times and difficult moments, but I just wanted more for myself. There were already four nurses in my family, and I didn't want to follow the same path. My mother was insistent on me staying in the medical field, so for a time, I did both jobs. When I finally burned out, I had to choose, and I chose my commission career over the stable paycheck and turned in my two weeks' notice. My family was sure I was setting myself up for failure, and fear kept me up at nights, but I had to do something to make a positive change in my life.

I worked for a couple years with that company, and they taught me more and more. I had a raging desire to keep learning, and I loved the opportunity to hand over house keys to people who had never believed they could own their own home. The satisfaction of turning dreams into reality was a blessing I could be a part of, and I hoped that experience would never end.

I was promoted several times, and my employer began to rely on me to be the top producer and to close his deals as well. He promised me certain commission but then disappeared when it was time to pay, and I began to feel like my whole world rested on the shoulders of that one individual. I began listening to account executives who continuously asked why I hadn't branched out on my own, as I was a top-notch producer who cared deeply about my clients. I contemplated their constant reassurances that I could do it and become very successful. My employer had diligently trained me, and he counted on me, but he also took advantage of me.

I prayed about it and decided to resign after the Christmas season. I gave my two weeks' notice and took that leap of faith to become my own boss. I studied and obtained my mortgage broker license, and I began the next chapter on my journey to success, hoping to build a future for me and my family, one with unlimited potential and possibilities.

I will always remember my first client, a single mother who wanted the experience, security, and stability of owning her own home for her and her son. When I placed the keys in her hands, tears rolled down her cheeks, and her son asked, "Is this really our own house?"

She exclaimed, "Yes! It is ours!"

The eight-year-old boy then ran over and hugged me so tight that I thought I wouldn't be able to ever breathe again. He said, "Because of you, Ms. Sharlene, we have our own home, and I can buy a 'Do not disturb' sign like my cousin's and put in on my door. They won't be able to kick me out, because this is *my* house and *my* room. This is the first time in my whole life that I will have my own room," he declared proudly.

Tears just fell from my eyes. I was truly touched, and I wanted to feel that over and over again. From then on, I would make sure my business did well, so I could experience that constantly. I finally felt a feeling of satisfaction, the one I'd been seeking, with the open door of growth and possibilities shining right in front.

Overall, life was great, even with its ups and downs, and I learned to roll with the punches of being a business owner in a new field. I learned through that process that only you have the power to materialize your hopes and dreams; there will be supporters of your vision, your goals, and your dreams, but there will also be naysayers and those who believe you are losing your mind for taking such a risk. I knew I didn't want to spend my life wandering and regretting, so I jumped and took the leap. I have been in this industry for over thirteen years, with a primary focus on growth in the real estate arena.

I must reiterate that if you are the smartest person in your group of friends or acquaintances, you definitely need to reevaluate and alter your group and your way of thinking. I have realized that if you truly want something in life, you have to go out and seek it. Faith without works is dead, so if we all follow our dreams regardless of a pass or fail grade, this world may just be a happier place full of much happier people.

Napoleon Hill shared a view for us to consider: Don't follow money. Follow your passion, and the money will follow in the end. One of the most courageous things to do in this world is to follow your passion with faith. Your commitment will turn your life around, because you will embrace life and take it by the reins. You will be the power source, the electricity of your own golden pathway to success.

This is the time to take your royalty mindset seat on your throne to success as you commit to greatness and believing in yourself. Today is the day when you should say, "No more procrastination, no more excuses, no more thinking that good things only happen for lucky folks and not me!" Today is the beginning of the rest of your life. Whatever dream is burning a hole in the pit of your belly, the time to let that fire burn and excel to the best you ever possible is now. The feeling of building a legacy for your children as you gain independence is a only truly explainable by the experience.

I remember listening to great businessmen speak about never getting rich working for other people. That was why they chose their own path. I strongly believe that we all have a purpose. That purpose is our buried treasure that resides deep in our being, and it was placed in each and every one of us by God. It is up to us to unveil that buried treasure, and once it is unveiled, our lives will be forever changed. We will open the doors to opportunity and release the map to our destiny as we commit to our own journey. No matter how rugged the terrain, we must be steadfast and committed to following our purpose and elevating our lives to our true success, by loving and believing in ourselves. We must remember to pray, plan, and proceed as we move forward. We all know when the time has come to move on. Listen to the voice and that burning sensation in your belly and give your two weeks' notice.

TELL THE WORLD WHAT YOU HAVE TO OFFER!

*N*ow you are ready to go full steam ahead and roll out your business! A word of advice that I received from another dear friend, Trevor Otts, is to "look for the seeds to spread more fruit as opposed to [looking for] the actual fruit." As consumers, it's easy for us to get caught up with the smaller things, Trevor's point is that we can grow many trees with those seeds, go worldwide, expand, and generate multiple streams of success. On the other hand, once a piece of fruit is eaten, it is no more. By planting trees, you can pluck multiple fruit and expect more each and every season. It is time for you to think as an entrepreneur, as an investor in yourself. When you do, things will turn around dramatically for you and your business.

This all goes back to investing in yourself so you will never go broke. Once you have an established goal, here is what you need:

1. Website
2. Business cards
3. A strong, thirty-second elevator pitch
4. Testimonials
5. A strong social media and Internet presence
6. A license to do business, if applicable (Check with your local Small Business Administration for more information)

Getting a website is a lot easier than you think. Many sites allow you to simply drag and click to create your own top-notch HTML site, or you can hire Peak Performers Institute to create a money-making website that truly speaks to your talents. Sometimes, staying in your lane will benefit you in the long run. The last thing you want to do as a business owner is to skimp on the important things. Your website should be updated as you grow; it should also be working at all times, because you never know when someone is going to check you out. The more you update and add key words, the higher it will rank on the popular search engines. The more you come up on Google or Bing, the more you will earn.

Business cards can make you or break you! I met Dr. Willie Jolley at Peak Performers Institute event, and I was so excited to give him one of my stellar, highly decorated cards. He looked at that little two-by-three card and said, "WOW! This sure is pretty, but if I cannot read it, what good is?" Talk about a reality check, but he was right. In fact, he gave me one of his million-dollar cards, and I saw the difference and will share it with you.

First, bold, bright colors will catch your customer's attention, forcing them to look at it. The font size and type must cater to your niche market. In my case, my market is over forty, and a high percentage rely on corrective lenses to assist with reading; my fancy calligraphy font would be a strain on their eyes. Also, include an action photo and a list of all you do as a professional. Again, you will have to spend in order to get your point across! The first thing people do when they get your business card is look on *both* sides. My mother always said; "A word to the wise is sufficient," so allow me to give you one: Make sure *your* information is printed on both sides of your business card, not the information from the company that manufactured those cards. Don't give someone else free advertising just so you can save; you will end up walking over dollars to pick up pennies, and that makes no cents—pun intended! A well-constructed card should have your name, company name, website, and phone number, all fully visible.

Your photo should be non-distracting, professional, and catered to your business. If you are a professional, be sure you are dressed that way in your photo. Maybe you are a more relaxed professional, like my friend Mack Burnett III, who will don a blazer, tie, button-up, nice jeans, and loafers or hard-bottoms. My friend Mario Price, Esq. is known for his elaborate bowties, and they would be missed if he was not wearing them, almost like Stacie NC Grant with her thirty-minute shoes. The point is that you should have a neat, clean-cut look. Make it your own, and then market it.

Your thirty-second elevator pitch must be clean, concise, and re-hearsed. You only get one shot to make a strong first impression. It should include a firm handshake, good eye contact, and answer why your business calls to the masses. The listener should know who you are, what you do, how you do it best, where you are located, when you are in operation, and—most of all—why you. Trust me, you are not the only motivational speaker, coach, writer, designer, driver, singer, or PR person in the world, so you must stand out as the best and make the person you are speaking to believe they will be missing out on some-thing great if they do not choose you. The pitch should end with a business card exchange; if you are given a card, look it over on the front and back. Appear interested, as you should be, and hold it in your hand until they walk away. Make a positive comment about the card, but do not shove it in your pocket or bag, as you will lose credibility. The last thing you want to do as an entrepreneur is appear to be selfishly disinterested.

Testimonials are a great way to get the word out about your business. In a sea of other small business owners, you need a way to surface for some fresh air. You may feel as though you are drowning in the successes of others, but instead of worrying about it, use it as your motivation. If you take your eyes off the island of success, you will drown. Figure out how to stay afloat and relevant. Find that target market you can speak to, and let them know how good you are. Soon, you will have dozens of referrals and kind comments to choose from, as long as you earn the words. Also return the favor, for there is enough business to go around. Be a professional! Acknowledge the good in others, and it will come back to you.

These days, it is easy to get caught up in and distracted by hashtags, tweets and timelines, but even in the world of social media, it is up to you to stay professional. If you want to showcase the kids and what you did last summer, do it on a separate page or account. When investors look for you and see games and updates on your favorite shows, they will not take you seriously; however, if they see positive updates and what you are doing pertaining to your business, your phone will go crazy!

Pick the right site to display what it is that you do. If you are consistent with automated posting, like the penny marketing tool (email me at info@awakethechampioninyou.org to learn more about this Peak Performers Institute amazing tool), it will post for you, with the right language on the right sites. Following the guide above will boost your SEO in your favor, and you'll soon be a household name.

One thing to remember is to stay fresh. Don't be redundant! There is a difference between networking and spamming. Ask permission before you post on others' pages, and use page etiquette. Phishing through people's accounts to gain celebrated acquaintances is not a good practice, nor is it good to tag anyone in your posts without an understanding, especially if you are in the same field of expertise. Another tip is to keep it professional and tasteful. Once it is released into cyber space, it is no longer able to be retracted; before you delete it, it's already been read thousands of times. Be wise.

Check with www.SBA.gov to learn about new opportunities for small business owners. They will direct you to your local office and determine if there are grants, RFPs or advice that will benefit your business. Best of all, it's free! Also, you may live in a state that requires you to incorporate, and it is better to be safe than sorry. The few moments you spend on their site can save you years of heartache and penalties.

Have faith, knowing that you've taken all the proper steps to get your name out there, and soon it will be time to benefit from all of your hard work.

I WONT GIVE UP!

Mitsie Robinson

*M*y three D's to achieve success are: determination, dedication, and devotion.

Put God first!

"Excuse me!" I said when my employer called me into the office. "I'm sorry, but did you just say you have to let me go?" I then stated, "I thought I was supposed to get a promotion." I had done what my job description entailed, even gone above and beyond my call of duty. I had even gone to a client's house at two in the morning when they passed away, when I was not on call. "I'm sorry, but did you say it's because I turned my progress notes in too late? I turned them in. You gave me and all the other employees, a week to complete them." I thought to myself, *Excuses, excuses, excuses, one after another.*

I got up, said a prayer, smiled, thanked him, and walked out the door with dignity. I was finally free from all the lies, the unprofessionalism, the unrealistic expectations, and the betrayal. *Thank you, Father God, for I am released!*

When I proceeded to the elevators, I heard a small, still voice say to me, "Don't worry. I have greater things in store for you!"

As I was leaving the building, I smiled, looked up to the sky, and said, "Thank you, Jesus!"

I was born and raised in South Bronx, New York, the youngest of eight. We lived in Jackson Projects, on welfare. To some people, this was a disgrace, and rumors circulated from block to block. Some of our neighbors said, "There are too many of them. They're gonna end up on drugs, not do anything with their lives." It was so funny to me, because they did not see what was going on in our apartment. There, between those walls, there was pure love, lots of laughter, rehearsals for singing in talent shows, and my mother constantly saying, "We will make it, by the grace of God. We are somebody."

On the other hand, there were many who loved us. We sang, played sports, played videogames, and kept busy with major, boot camp-style chores; even our friends were put to work when they came over, but they actually looked forward to it. We were the Robinsons, and we always had a lot of fun and could do anything, as long as it was positive.

I sang and sang. I loved to sing and was well known around the block and at school, but I always new that even if I became a singer, I'd have to have a fallback plan.

Because of my love for people and going to church as a child with my family, I knew what God wanted me to do. I had a special gift for spreading love and helping others. I love to care, listen to people, and provide advice when I can. At an early age, I was already problem-solving, helping my community. It was not a challenge for me; it just came naturally, and I knew it was a blessing.

At the age of thirteen, while in eighth grade at PS 151 Lou Gehrig Junior High, I knew what I wanted to do. I wanted to become a nurse, since nurses always had to exhibit a desire to care for and help others. I went to the studio to lay tracks for my album, and I managed to juggle school and my dearest hobby; to this day, I still sing, except only in the shower. I decided to go to Jane Adams Vocational High School, where I could be a nursing major, and I loved it. I'd always had a drive to do better, to go straight to the top, and I was determined.

As I approached the end of my junior year, with great academic grades, my producer for my singing career reached out to my parents and me, telling me that Def Jam Records was interested in signing me to their label. It was great news, a huge opportunity for me. A stage crop was built. I took album pictures and went to dance class and vocal coaching once a week. I was told I would be the opening act for The O'Jays, and I was filled with so much happiness and excitement. We cried tears of joy and praised God: "In the name of Jesus, thank you, Lord!"

Since it was the end of eleventh grade for me, they were going to pull me out of school and let me finish my senior year on the road, touring with a tutor. I had to give it great thought and consideration. I wanted to graduate with my friends, so I had a choice to make. As a young adult, my parents let me make that decision, with the guarantee of their continued support, whatever choice I made. Although it was a tough decision because of my love for music, my final thought was to follow my ultimate dream of entrepreneurship. I chose to go to Delaware State College in 1988 and accomplish my goal of going straight to the top. I was dedicated.

Obstacles

"I'm sorry, but did you say I don't qualify for financial aid?" I looked at my mother and stepfather in shock.

The problem was that my mother and I had just moved in with him in Jamaica, Queens, New York. As the youngest sibling, I was last to leave home. My mother instantly felt guilty and began to cry. I told her it was okay, that I would make a way.

I took out a student loan and went to school. I stayed in my room for practically my whole freshman and sophomore years—just studying, with no parties or homecoming. In my junior year, during my clinical rotation, I was extremely interested in psychology. That year, I confirmed again that I would someday be my own boss. I was confident and wanted to achieve the best academic grades possible. In 1991, I was certified as a member of the Honors Program. In 1992, I was chosen to be included in *Who's Who Among Students in American Universities and Colleges for Outstanding Merit and Accomplishment.* I graduated in 1993 with a bachelor's of science and passed my nursing boards examination on the first try.

I started working the very next month and immediately had a house built. It was a very proud moment for me and my family. I was excited. I was the youngest to graduate with a bachelor's and buy a house, and I was happy to be an example for my family. Yes, we can do anything, as long as we put God first.

Throughout my journey, many obstacles tried to hold me back. I was bullied a lot, from grade school right on up through college, for no reason. I didn't want to go back in the past by fighting and being jumped, but I had to defend myself. My siblings helped, but they were not around most of the time. I fought by myself, and I was getting better at it.

I lost a ton of so-called friends for no apparent reason. This may sound silly and immature, but it was true, even in college. There was a lot of peer pressure around me in my freshman year of college, and eventually, everyone just stopped talking to me. I called my mother in tears, begging to come home. It was torture.

During that same time, some of my relatives passed away, and I could not make it to their funerals. My personal relationship of seven years had gone sour, and a very special friend of mine had fallen into some train tracks back in the Bronx, resulting in his paralysis. All of these grim life events took place while I was facing several personal challenges of my own. Still, even when things were starting to wear me down, I kept telling myself, "I won't give up! I'm going to the top. I will not stop. I will have my own nursing business very soon and be able to help people in the community, despite any obstacle I encounter." I was devoted.

I soon married and gave birth to two sons, my little blessings. I started a nursing staffing agency, but I was unable to gain the client contracts I wanted, and it did not work out. I had made my first attempt to become an entrepreneur, only to be disappointed.

After giving some thought to what I needed to do to achieve my goal, I thought of a way to help the community again. I saw heartbroken, hurting, hopeless, helpless, hungry, homeless people in the world. My heart ached for them and their struggles, and I had to do something.

In 2001, I went to Wesley College to pursue an advanced degree as a clinical nurse specialist in health promotion and illness prevention. I knew the degree would allow me to be a clinical expert, consultant, educator, and researcher in the community.

In 2003, I graduated with honors and was inducted into Sigma Theta Tau Honor Society. I was the only African American scholar in my class, and it was a huge achievement. Not only did I receive grants for my advanced degree, but it was another ladder step to get me to where I wanted to be. I am more than a conqueror.

After receiving my master's degree, I worked on a psychiatric unit. I was the supervisor for Clinical Services. I had a bigger house built, but at the same time, I was going through a lengthy divorce. It was a troubling time, and I was not happy. I felt like I was being held hostage, like another obstacle was trying to hold me back. I knew it was not healthy for me, our sons, or my career, so after nine years of marriage, I had to let go.

I worked for years at a temp nursing agency, which allowed flexibility, and I was given the opportunity to make my own schedule. That was great, because I did not want to commit to anyone or any healthcare organizations, to build someone else's career as I'd done in the past. I stayed focused and disciplined to achieve my dream. I'd always been a hard worker, so I knew I could just as hard to be a successful entrepreneur. That was my ultimate goal.

I wanted to consult with mental health and substance abuse clients, so I finally took a position at the biggest hospital in Delaware, Christiana. I thought my position as a crisis intervention nurse would be an opportunity that could assist with my dream, so I reached out and grabbed it.

At that point in my career, I was making power moves to get where I wanted to be. My position had a lot of responsibilities and provided great opportunities for the community. I took part in helping a client reach their goals, and I was very proud that I helped make a positive change in someone's life. It was so gratifying, as I loved helping others. That was God's gift for me. I wanted to make the best of it. I wanted to be someone's hope when they felt hopeless, someone's help when they felt no one cared.

My position allowed me to consult with the community, people who were in need of support and wanted a change or to recover from something negative in their past, such as suicidal thoughts, mental health issues, or substance abuse. I provided crisis intervention for all ages, health/wellness promotion, illness prevention, individual/family consultation, grief/loss support, traumas, anger management, PTSD, and mood disorders, just to name a few. I knew the job would help me gain the skills and knowledge to push me closer to my dream, my vision of becoming an entrepreneur.

As I explained earlier, I lost a healthcare position that promised a promotion. Unfortunately, it did not turn out that way. It was okay, though, because had I not lost that job, I probably would not have become an entrepreneur. As the R&B artist Fantasia says in her hit song, "Sometimes you have to lose to win again," and I won!

Why entrepreneurship?

This question is simple for me to answer. I did not want to work for anyone else, someone who would take my hard work for granted while I helped them accomplish their dream. I had helped to build others' dreams while neglecting my own. I knew I would not let myself down if I was my own boss. I wanted to be free to make my own choices, my own schedule. I did not want to be restricted or tied down when I had family emergencies, and I did not want to feel bad for having to leave work. I have always believed God must be first, family second, and career third.

Not only did I want to work in the community, but I wanted to be part of the community, helping people. It is my desire to be a vessel of love, peace, and hope, bearing fruit for the Lord. Yes, I consider my practice as a ministry for all. My doors never close. This is one of the many benefits of entrepreneurship. I am the decision-maker, problem-solver, and change agent.

What does it mean to put God first?

Before making a heavy or difficult decision about anything, I talk to God for guidance. Whoever you choose your higher inspiration to be, trust and believe in it. Go to that spirit, and make sure to have a personal connection. Make a conscious effort to be open to suggestions and discipline. To grow spiritually, it is imperative that you avoid being easily offended. Wisdom from your higher inspiration and like-minded people will make you stronger, not hurt you. It is important that you believe, trust, and have faith in what you are doing if you are going to make a recovery from your old uncomfortable ways.

I chose my path to success.

I chose my own path to success, and it started with identifying and assessing what I wanted to do in life. Take a piece of paper and divide it into two columns. Label one column with "Pros" and the other with "Cons." Then write down your advantages (pros), and your disadvantages (cons). Be honest with yourself, and document your strengths and weaknesses. This exercise will assist you in making a decision. If you are unsure, write down a couple career choices, and do the same exercise. Hopefully, you will identify career options that you will enjoy doing.

Do your research. After narrowing down your anticipated career choices, vision, and dream, put it into action; create an action plan. This format is a lot like the nursing process. Assess your selected career choices/opportunities. If you don't know what those are, just start writing down what you enjoy doing and what you hope to accomplish. This process may take longer than anticipated; however, it is sure to give you some direction in someday owning your own business as a entrepreneur. Find out your needs to achieve in order to get where you would like to be, with measurable goals.

Implement your plan by researching your career interest. Look at school websites, literature reviews, journals, networking opportunities, and school history. Visit different schools that offer classes or courses in what you would like to do.

Evaluate whether you have achieved your goals to begin a journey of success. If you are dissatisfied with your results, go back to your goals. Allow yourself additional time if necessary. Do not be discouraged! This exercise may take a little more time, especially if you are still uncertain regarding your choices. Be encouraged to empower yourself. Sometimes we have to go back to square one to achieve results.

My final advice.

Stay focused on your passion, vision, and dream. Remember to make a conscious effort to discipline yourself to achieve your goal of becoming your own boss, an entrepreneur. Try to network with people who can assist you in achieving your goal. Building healthy support systems and relationships is a must.

Stay in school. Research the amount of education necessary to begin your journey. Remember your purpose, be confident, and try to develop patience while doing so. Do not rush through this. Remember, you want positive results, and that will require sacrifices. If you spend more time developing your plan for success, you will spend less time trying to fix mistakes. Try to follow your destiny, and also try to stay motivated.

Do not give up. Do not stop believing. Stay full of hope and expectation. God's power is limitless, and He'll breakthrough for you. Follow your dream!

Feel free to use the three D's to achieve, as well as inspirational quotes from brainyquote.com to get you motivated.

Determination. We all have dreams. In order to make dreams come into reality, it takes an awful lot of determination, dedication, self-discipline, and effort. You can do it. Persistence and determination alone are omnipotent.

Dedication. Keep your dreams alive. Understand that to achieve anything requires faith, and belief in yourself. It also requires vision, hard work, determination, and dedication. Remember, all things are possible for those who believe. If you believe in yourself and have dedication and never quit, you'll be a winner. The price of victory is high, but so are the rewards.

Devotion. Loyalty and devotion leads to bravery. Bravery leads to the spirit of self-sacrifice. To succeed in your mission, you must have single-minded devotion to your goal. With faith, discipline, and selfless devotion on duty, there is nothing worthwhile that you cannot achieve.

Since I began to write this, I've added another important D:

Discipline. Discipline is the bridge between goals and accomplishment. To discipline is to control one's own mind. If one can control their own mind, he/she can find the way to success, enlightenment, and wisdom. With self-discipline most anything is possible.

In conclusion, I pray that I have encouraged, and touched many lives with my journey to success. I hope I have influenced others to follow their dream. Being an entrepreneur requires hard work, sacrifice, dedication, and self-belief. Remember to stay focused, and keep your eyes on the prize. Speak your own business into existence. At the end of your journey, you will reap the reward.

Try to stay tuned with community events, and indulge yourself in helping others. Tell people about your journey to inspire them. Give hope to the hopeless, provide help for the helpless and spread love and comfort to the heartbroken. Research shelters for the homeless and food for the hungry.

Remember, being successful as an entrepreneur depends on one person: you!

God bless!

MY JOURNEY TO ENTREPRENEURSHIP

Dwijesh A. Ramnath

*W*hy do we do the tasks we are presented with everyday? The routines, the conversations, and the way we think and present ourselves? Is it because we are just trying to survive, to make ends meet, to live comfortably? Or is it because we enjoy what we do and we choose to undertake each task so we can grow, develop, mature, and move one step closer to our dreams. That is what separates an entrepreneur from a person who is living just to survive: the burning desire to accomplish your dreams, reach your financial goals, and acquire those luxuries in life. Very often, we settle for the term J.O.B. security, but no job is guaranteed. If you want to achieve your dreams, you must be an entrepreneur rather than a worker. Dreams rely on you becoming different, challenging the ways of society.

My name is Dwijesh A. Ramnath, and I am from Johannesburg, South Africa, I am an entrepreneur, author, motivational speaker, dancer,. and founder of the self-help, nonprofit organization, Power of a Teen. Entrepreneurship incorporates a way of life or me. As an entrepreneur, the way you think, speak, learn and challenge yourself is important to your success. If you are not setting goals that challenge you and bring out the best in you, then you are not growing yourself.

The Beginning

My journey as an entrepreneur started with very humble and small beginnings. Ever since I was a child, I had a desire to become an entrepreneur, a risk-taker, and a successful person in life.

It all began back in my primary school days. The very first time I set up my own business, a retail business at an annual school entrepreneurship event, I was excited. I was only thirteen, and I had no idea how to run or manage a business, but I took the time to learn the basic principles before the event. I also came up with an idea for a product so unique that seven years later, it is still being used, a sports shirt that displayed the fifty-year commemoration of the school.

Through understanding the basic principles, I managed to run my business in such a way that I had generated 200 percent profits in preorders a week before the actual event. It was then that I fell in love with the idea of being different, the idea of conjuring ideas and turning ideas into solid profit.

To be an entrepreneur, one must have the ability to learn. Why many people fail as entrepreneurs simply arises from the fact that they are not willing to learn more than what they already know. My first venture took more learning than actual implementation, but that first step in learning grew me, modeled me, and gave me knowledge that will always be used in entrepreneurship. That hunger for learning is what drove me to success.

Eventually, I realized that learning is somewhat of an art form. The more knowledge I absorbed, the better my strokes, my flow, and my masterpiece became. I still remember those basic principles, and they help me to this day.

Understanding Failure as a Means to Learn

I have failed many times in life, and I didn't grow up with wealth. I spent my childhood in below-average economic conditions, a place of poverty, a place where people were so boxed into their mindsets, and thinking was constricted by the brutal environment.

My mindset and thinking, however, were above average. My grades in school, my mental focus, mental drive, and ability to act and carry my ideas forward were not average. When I turned fourteen years old, I realized that I had to transfer what I visualized mentally into physical form. I was achieving excellence in school, manifesting my beautiful ideas into the physical life I was living, but it was not easy. I failed many times in this process.

In my high school days I went through a cycle, emotionally, spiritually, mentally, and physically; it was a time filled with highs and lows, victory and failure. At seventeen, at another school entrepreneurship event, I once again had the opportunity to test my abilities and push myself to the limits. This time, my goal was to create a business that would supersede the profits and marketing of all the other participants' projects.

Learning is so important, and that was exactly what I did. I learned systems to sales and marketing principles that would help me achieve my business goal. Day and night, I worked, learned, and created my systems and operations. To no surprise, I ended up generating more profit than anyone else. Still, the journey resides in the experiences through failures as well as past success. I worked that idea into a plan so sound that every year at the high school event, the business continues to succeed; even after I graduated high school, I kept collecting royalties.

Entrepreneurship means being able to grow stronger from failure, learning to implement stronger tactics. I was prepared to fail in my high school days as an entrepreneur, but I kept pushing to succeed. Not every idea of mine turned out successful, but those that did, I worked hard on, day in and day out. I left no stone unturned.

But what did I learn in the process of failure? I learned strength, character, courage, heart, and spirit. Little did I know that my greatest challenge was yet to come; I didn't see it coming, and when it hit, it crashed into me full force, like a massive tidal wave. I found myself swimming in the deep, and it eventually became a make-or-break situation for me.

Finding a Reason to Hold On and Becoming Determined to Succeed

When I graduated from high school, I went back to a state of being broke. Everything I had worked so hard for was lost. I had no money to study or to pay for shelter or food, and it was like being poor all over again. The situation became so bad that I forgot what it was like to be an entrepreneur, and I opted for a J.O.B

I worked and slaved away day in and day out, struggling every day, cycling long distances, working long hours, and hating every minute, just to earn an income to survive. I had to ask myself, *Why am I working at a job I do not like, working at a job that makes me sick and still doesn't earn enough to pay my expenses?* I was literally in a make-or-break situation at eighteen years of age.

Finally, one day, I decided that enough was enough, and I fell back into the mindset of an entrepreneur. For some reason, this time was different. It was not about money or living a wonderful lifestyle. Rather, it was more about the art of entrepreneurship, about accomplishing the so-called impossible and using my skills and knowledge to help others achieve their dreams. I took a stand and quit that J.O.B. to become a better and more phenomenal entrepreneur than I had ever been before.

On the verge of losing my housing, I conjured up the courage, strength, and determination to succeed in a business that was greater than anything I had tackled before.

Property

Giving up a nine-to-five to work on what you desire is way better than being a worker for someone else

Just as before, I went back to what I'd done from the beginning: learning. Getting into the property business was not easy, and furthermore, I had no clue how the business operated. I learned and implemented as much information as I could, but I did not have much time; it was a matter of having a place to sleep or being homeless, and if I did not commit entirely to my goal, I would not have a roof over my head.

In a market that was not doing well, that had more sellers than buyers and a low rent-to-mortgage ratio, I developed a system that guaranteed sustainable income. It also made housing affordable to those with very little money to spend. My first property investment, $200, boomed into a passive income of $2,000 per month, all because I'd created a system that allowed a small investment to produce a large monthly return, as well as assets with infinite annual return potential.

It was my first project as an entrepreneur in a larger world, and I achieved great success. At nineteen, I was approached by business and property owners who wanted to know how I'd done it. Before long, local newspapers and radio stations were contacting me for interviews. Everyone seemed to be amazed by my abilities and the system I had created.

The Limitless Power of Being an Entrepreneur

Hungry to learn and grow and develop my art form, I began to attend seminars, workshops, and courses hosted by some of the wealthiest entrepreneurs in the world. At that point, I decided to take entrepreneurism one step further and build my very own organization to help teenagers become entrepreneurs and find success for themselves. Entrepreneurship was my art, and I wanted to share it.

The Need for Help in a Rough Economy

Over time, I learned that the biggest problem people face in becoming an entrepreneur is what step to take first. I was determined to help others, and my desire changed from generating profit and wealth to helping people become the best they can be. When I ventured into the self-help industry, I had little understanding about how it operated, but I had never let that stop me before, and I wouldn't let it stop me then. I knew my market, and I wanted to be different. I wanted to offer something unique in self-help, something the average teen and young adult would be able to relate to, something that would help them become phenomenal, so Power of a Teen was born.

From a Twitter account, to a Facebook page, to a book, and eventually an organization, Power of a Teen started to grow and became better known within the community and schools. It was more about helping than the money made from helping, so we decided to go to nonprofit. The team consists of teenagers who have achieved success in entrepreneurship.

That is the beauty of being an entrepreneur: You have the ability to make a change in this world, to help people, to help the economy, and to grow yourself in the process. No matter what, I stuck to every goal and achieved my dreams. Now, I thoroughly enjoy what I do, and I am always learning, growing, and developing and helping others to do the same. My motto is, "Always a student, never a master."

Ultimately, it came down to willpower. I had to make a change and become different, achieve financial freedom, escape the rat race, achieve my dreams, and help people. My journey was not easy. It was lonely, at times, heartbreaking and sad, but along the way, I failed and got back up. It's not easy getting back up, but when it is do or die, you find a way to become a warrior. Ultimately, I developed into one. I gave up being normal, gave up that nine-to-five, and entered a world where my ideas are not limited, where I can be myself. That world is the world of an entrepreneur.

Be a Boss!

There are few myths and negative assumptions about entrepreneurs that often discourage people from trying to become one. Some of these common misconceptions are:

- Only rich people have the ability to become entrepreneurs.
- I do not have the skills to be an entrepreneur.
- I need to be older to understand what it takes to be an entrepreneur.
- I am scared of failing.
- Only a certain race of people can be wealthy.

The list is endless, but the truth is that entrepreneurism is color-blind. It takes no notice of your skin color, status, age, or current skill set. If anything, being self-employed is the best decision anyone can make. You do not have to conform to the norms of society; you can be different and think differently. Consider that Apple was very different as compared to any other computer technology company. Facebook was different, something new, and now these companies are two of the most successful in the world, a common household word in homes worldwide. They had no fear of being different and original. That is exactly what is so brilliant about being an entrepreneur.

There are so many reasons why entrepreneurship is so much better than a nine-to-five job:

- Entrepreneurism is an art form. There are no limits on the ideas you present, the ideas you implement, or how you will turn those ideas into a success.

- Being an entrepreneur is a constant learning process. As an entrepreneur, you will learn far more on a daily basis than a worker sitting in a job will learn in a month.

- There are no boundaries. Entrepreneurs do not set boundaries. Their achievement and goals are limitless, whether those goals are financial, vision based, or strategic.

- The world will be your playground. Rather than working for the world, you will start to see opportunities everywhere you go. It eventually gets to the point where you start to play and experiment with far more opportunities than you ever dreamt possible.

- Work is not work; it is your play time. Becoming an entrepreneur means you do what you enjoy and turn it into a sustainable business. This, in essence, becomes your playtime rather than work.

Again, the list is endless, but keep in mind that ultimately, you define the success of your entrepreneurial career. There are many ways to reach your dreams when you are an entrepreneur, but how many ways can you reach your dreams as an employee? Entrepreneurism does not see age, color, race, or creed. It is all about ambition and willpower. There is no room for fear! Dedication, passion, determination, and hard work crowns success at the end of the road. Are you willing to run toward it or leave it?

GOING FROM YOUR BROWN BOX TO YOUR NEXT

Nisha Ray

*I*f you've ever worked in corporate America, you understand the feeling of seeing security walk by your cubicle with a brown box in hand. Everyone holds his or her breath, wondering who's going to get the axe. The whispering starts up as co-workers try to figure out where security will stop: "You know, she's never on time… He messed up that big deal last week… They only hired her because she was sleeping with the boss."

That brown box is the sign in corporate America that someone's life is going to go a little differently than they realized that morning, and until that box stops at the unfortunate one's desk, a million worrisome thoughts fly through everyone's head: *Are they coming to my desk? Are they going to the desk of a co-worker?* The dread that fills everyone and the prayers that fly up are the same everywhere, no matter what company you work for. There are sighs of relief from those who were passed by, and the person with the box on their desk is overcome with panic.

What do you go through in the quiet hours when there is no one there but you and God? How are you impacted emotionally, financially, and spiritually while transitioning from your brown box to your next? How do you keep your faith and keep moving forward to your next? What do you have in you to get you to your next? What if I told you that this period of unknowing is to be celebrated and embraced?

Would you believe that, or would you think I must come from money or that I'm just fronting? Would you even consider that such a statement would come from a single mom of three who has gone through the struggles? Probably not. But that is exactly who it's coming from.

I have been there, a single mother, with a brown box on my desk. Forgive me, but at that time, I wasn't where I am now, so my first thought was, *Oh sh*t! What the heck am I gonna do? My rent needs to be paid, along with my daughter's daycare bill. I have sacrificed so much for this company, made them so much money, and now they're coming at me like this!* Little did I know at that time that I should have kissed the security guard and manager and thanked them. I should have jumped up and done a little happy dance on top of my desk. On the way out the door, I should have proudly thrown up my two fingers and said, "Deuces!"

Yes, you read that right. I should have gotten up on that desk and done a Jerry Maguire and said, "Who is going with me?" I should have done a Coyote Ugly move, mixed with some *Happy Feet,* and said, "Thank you, God, for answering my prayer and moving me when I did not know how to move myself." If you are going through this right now and have just lost your job or been out of work for a long time, give God some praise. Thank Him and ask Him to bless those who let you go, because in doing so, they just made room in your life for God to move.

As I study people and look at myself and the things that hold us back, I find that there is one big similarity: the need for security and to hold on to that safety net. I knew God was calling me for more and wanted to do more in my life, but I limited myself because I needed that steady paycheck. I did not know how to rely on God to be my provider, to make sure I had what I needed, even when it seemed impossible. When your benefit package or unemployment runs out, how do you hold on? When you look at your kids' feet and see that they are in desperate need of shoes and you don't even have enough money for food, how can you trust God then? It's an uncomfortable place to be when you have no clue how you're going to make it from day to day.

When there is no more security, no more comfort, how can you stand on the fact that God told you He has plans to prosper you, especially when it looks like the whole world is out for your demise? What if I told you that security can be a trap from the enemy to hold you back from God's true plans for you? Yes, security and comfort can be a trap. It can keep you in a situation that seems okay or may even seem great, but it may not be the best God can do in your life or through you. It's just comfortable, and that's not the most important thing.

God kept calling me to deeper levels in Him, especially when I didn't know what the day would bring. I had no idea if someone would call with a job or if the money would come for the rent. God was teaching me how to trust Him. He was teaching me faith on a whole different level, teaching me how not to allow my situations to determine my outlook and my disposition. Not only did He teach me faith in Him, but He also taught me to have faith in the skills and talents He gifted me with. God is called Jehovah Jireh for a reason: He provides everything we need—every talent, every resource, and even the faith and strength to get through our day and to get to our next.

I bet you are wondering why I keep talking about your next. What I have discovered in my journey is that with every trial, there is a next you are supposed to get to. I lost my job, and I've also lost homes, cars, and money. There have been times when I didn't know how I was going to diaper my baby. What I did not realize in those times was that all that I was going through would put me in a position to understand the lack single mothers have when they do not have money or resources coming in. It allowed me to completely understand the quiet suffering of the children of single parents. Years later, that knowledge allowed me to start Heart for Single Moms through my ministry, Faith that Endures. We now provide diapers, wipes, bread, and even bicycles to children of single parents in our local community. The ministry was not something that happened immediately after losing my job; that job loss was only the catalyst God wisely used to keep moving me toward the purpose He created me for.

Losing my job meant I had to learn how to pamper myself and my daughter on a low budget or even no budget. I learned how to do home facials, how to mix oils, and now I am working on my Focus on You w/Nisha Ray Bath and Body Products. Again, this is something that has been years in the making. Every time I went through a loss of income, I couldn't complain, because I knew God put so much in me. I like to restore furniture, to make bath products and candles, and to write. There are so many books and products inside of me that when I am broke, I have no right to complain. God gave me everything I need not just to survive but to thrive. I won't be held captive by anyone's time schedule or job requirements because he gave me the capability to go out and start my own.

During this process, I had to learn how to let go of my fears, let go of my doubts and my need to try to meet other people's expectations for me. I spent hours praying and asking God to show me what my next was. I asked Him to take away the things within me that were limiting me and to provide me with the opportunities and direction He wanted me to go. It was really a case of being careful what I asked for, because God allowed my comfort zone to be taken away so I could no longer play it safe. I could no longer hide in the background. He put me up front and center. He stretched me and continues to stretch me so far that I know it has to be Him. Not only am I coaching and creating bath products, but I have also turned *Focus on You w/Nisha Ray* into a TV Talk show. The best part is that He did all of this in the midst of me being evicted from my apartment, when my finances were at their lowest point.

So thank your boss for firing you, and even if you don't want to do the dance on top of the desk, keep your cool, shake their hand, and dance down the parking lot when no one else is watching. Why shouldn't you? God is about to do something major in your life, as long as you are willing to step out into the unknown and trust Him.

How do you trust Him during this transition to your next? Belief is the first step. You must believe that He is a perfect parent. He is better than any human parent, and if a human parent wants the best for their child, wouldn't a perfect God want the best for His? Stand on His words and promises.

My favorite scripture to mediate on when things do not look as they should is Jeremiah 29:11 (KJV): "For I know the thoughts that I think toward you, saith the Lord, thoughts of peace and not of evil, to give you an expected end." I meditate on this scripture nonstop. If God has plans to prosper me and not to harm, that means everything is going to work out for me to get me to where God wants me to go.

Losing your job was meant to hurt you mentally, to break your confidence, to make things tight financially and more difficult spiritually. Thank God that He has given you confidence to know that you have an expected end.

Maybe you are asking, "Nisha, what about my finances? How do I get through without money?" Trust God! Start telling people what you are looking to do. Start speaking those dreams into existence, the ones you've been allowing to lie dormant in your spirit for so long; it's time to give birth to them. What talents do you have that can go from being merely a hobby to being a sustainable business?

Discover your talents. Ask your friends and family what they think you are naturally gifted to do. Ask yourself, *What would I do if money was not a issue?* What do you find yourself doing now for free?

For me, the answer to this last question was coaching and helping people. As I thought about it and reviewed my résumé and considered all my work experience, I realized that God had really put me through a unique training program. Be it in manufacturing, mortgages, and real estate, I was always helping people with trying to figure out their next step in life, as well as identifying things in the companies' processes that could be streamlined for better efficiency. So, when it was time for me to figure out my next, coaching was it. Again, this is real life, so it was not a simple process. First, I decided to go to real estate school, because I really didn't put much stock in being a life coach. Again, God turned me back around and allowed my path to be cleared so I can be here, coaching and writing this to help you figure out your next.

As you are looking to determine your next, look back over your career and hobbies. What stands out? What can be used for your business, a better position, or to start a new career altogether? After you answer these questions you will have a clearer view of what your next is? Take your time ask God to show you what He has for you and to give you the strategy and the resources to get to where He is leading you. Don't rush this process. Take your time, because what God has for you is already yours.

After you've discovered your next, how do you get there? You get out of your way and you keep moving on your journey by discovering what holds you back. What are your weaknesses? For me, one was allowing life to distract me. When storms came into my life, I paid more attention to what was going around me rather than to where I was going. My storms distracted me from the big picture of what I was trying to accomplish. I wanted to work for myself, and the money wasn't there. I figured I'd just have to get a job where I'd be unfulfilled and only make enough to barely get by, but that would not leave me enough energy and time to work on my business. I had to recognize that I could not make crack addict decisions, those that only relate to the moment and what you are going through, decisions that will only give you immediate gratification and no long-term benefits. I say this loosely, as I need to make it clear that I have never been on crack!

I also had to learn not to procrastinate. When something needed to get done, I had to just get it done. I also had to stop looking for validation and encouragement for others during my journey. The amazing things is that once I stopped doing those things or when I had to fight the urge to do them, God always stepped in. His perfect timing allowed me to get things done in a timely fashion, and when I stopped looking for encouragement or validation from others, He always provide those after His own heart to shower me with support and motivation and encouragement, all for His glory.

Look for God's glory and His blessing. Ezekiel 20:14 (NIV) says, "But for the sake of my name, I did what would keep it from being profaned in the eyes of the nations in whose sight I had brought them out." I have been through so much during my journey that I have made a decision to stop looking at the problems and start looking for the solutions. A big factor in finding the solutions is understanding that everything ultimately happens for God's glory. There are so many Bible stories of people trusting in God and being blessed in the midst of their mess. God told the Israelites that He did not bring them out for their sake; rather, it was for His name's sake, His glory. If you love God and proclaim His name, He will show up and show off in your life—not because you are so great but because He is. He will show Himself to be Jehovah, Jehovah Jireh, Jehovah Nissi, Jehovah Rappa: my provider, banner, and healer.

As you go through the task of figuring out what your next steps are, keep watching for God is get the glory out of your situation. Keep honoring and praising Him through every trial and hardship. Understand that whatever you are going through, God has already delivered you from it; it is just up to you to keep the faith until your situation looks likes the promise He gave you.

The road to your next may not be an easy one, but the reward will be great. God has put something inside you, and He made you special and unique for a reason. Everything He does is for a reason, for His glory. What has He designed you for? What is your purpose? How can you losing your job turn into your victory party? Is this your time to find your next dream job, go back to school, start your own business or nonprofit organization? I cannot answer these questions for you, but I can tell you that losing your job can be the best thing that has ever happened to you, as long as you put 100 percent of your energy into turning it into a positive and exploring these questions. Take it from a single mother of three who has been evicted and has experienced hardships: God will bring you everyone and everything you need to get to your next. Have faith and keep pushing!

The following page is a free tool from Bible.org. Use it to help you discover who God is, and mediate on the roles He can and will play through your journey called life. Remember, we have all been there and are all going through our own things. As the children of the most high God, everything in this world is ours; we simply need to stand in our authority and wait for God to say when it is time for the tides to shift and for us to receive our inheritance. Do not give up on Him, because I promise you that He will never give up on you!

FROM THE SERIES: BOOK D: BUILDING ON YOUR FOUNDATION

The Compound Names of Jehovah: Jireh, Rapha, Nissi (Session 60)

Purpose: There is no better way to discover what God is like than to look at His names. In the names considered in this material, we seek to understand how He cares for us.

Objectives
1. You will understand how God provides for our needs.
2. You will understand and learn to trust Him to make bitter things sweet.
3. You will learn to lean on Him and trust Him when the battle seems more than you can handle.

Scripture Memory
The Lord is good - indeed, he is a fortress in time of distress, and he protects those who seek refuge in him.
Nahum 1:7

Agenda
1. Mutual prayer and accountability.
2. Share Scripture memory.
3. Discuss questions.
4. Discuss any new terms.

Worksheet
JEHOVAH - JIREH: THE LORD WHO PROVIDES
GENESIS 22

1. Read the text carefully and answer the following questions.
    a. What was the setting for the revelation of this name of God?
    b. What made this especially difficult for Abraham? See
       Genesis 15:1-6; Genesis 21:1-6; Romans 4:18-22.
    c. Did Abraham really think he was going to have to take the
       life of his son Isaac? Genesis 22:5; Hebrews 11:17-19
    d. How was this story something like the story of Jesus and the
       offering of Calvary? See Genesis 22:2, 5, 6-9.

The Revelation of the Name Jehovah-Jireh, Genesis 22:12-14. The
meaning of this name is The Lord Who Provides. The name is literally,
The Lord Who Sees, or The Lord Who Will See To It. This is what we
long for when we have a need that is personal and special; One who
will see to our needs and provide for us. This is what Jehovah-Jireh
means; the Lord Who will see to it that my every need is met. One
Who knows my need because He sees. One Who is able to meet my
need in just the right time as He did for Abraham, and One Who can
meet it fully. For Abraham, it was the ram caught in the thicket that
was offered in Isaac's place. For us it is whatever we need.

2. Look up the sample verses and see the bountiful provision the
    Father has made for you and me. Write the meaning of each
    verse.
    a. Matthew 6:25-34
    b. Philippians 4:19
    c. Psalm 37:4
    d. Psalm 37:25
    e. Romans 8:37
    f. Ephesians 1:3

The name Jehovah-Jireh is a name that is crucial for us today as we seek to know the Father. It is a name that assures us that our Heavenly Father is able to provide any need we have. Trust Him for that!

JEHOVAH - RAPHA: THE LORD WHO HEALS
EXODUS 15:22-26

1. Read the text carefully and answer the following questions.
    a. What was the occasion for the revelation of this name of God?
    b. What exhilarating experience did Israel just have? Exodus 14:21-31
    c. What in our lives today can be likened to the bitter waters of Marah?
    List two or three "bitter" experiences you have endured recently.
    (1)
    (2)
    (3)
    d. The common way to approach a difficulty or stress in our life is the same way that the Israelites approached their stress, Exodus 15:24. Also see Job 2: 9. How do you usually approach difficulty that seems cruel to you?

2. The Revelation of the Name, Jehovah-Rapha, Exodus 15:25. Please note that the solution to this problem of bitter water was not one from the mind of Moses. It was rather from the Lord Himself.
    The Lord showed Moses a _____.
    The tree made the difference in the taste of the water. When we think of the many bitter experiences of life, what tree has made a difference? _____ Surely in the light of Calvary, the "tree makes a difference," the bitter problems of life can become sweet. Exodus 15:26 gives us the

revelation of the name. God says in the last part of the verse, "...I the Lord Am Your Healer." Literally, I am Jehovah-Rapha, the Lord Who makes bitter things sweet.

3. The name Jehovah-Rapha is a name that speaks to us and our need today. We live in a stressful world and society. Every day new problems confront us and we bend under the load of seemingly unsolvable problems. How can Jehovah-Rapha bring healing to a sick world. List some of the ways you already know that make this a reality for you.

    a.

    b.

    c.

4. Now look up the following verses and see if you can add anything to your list of practical ways to handle bitterness.

    a. Romans 8:28-29

    When will ultimate healing take place?

    Remember that God lives in eternity, and we in time. We are often in a hurry. God is never in a hurry. But the bitterness in our life will someday be made sweet. We have that promise.

    b. Hebrews 12:10-11

    How does "bitter chastisement" become sweet?

    This suggests that I need to view _____ in a positive way. It produces a _____ of _____ and _____.

    c. And what is the factor that makes a difference in the life of a child of God as compared with one who has not chosen the Savior? See John 1:12

    A tree provided by God made the difference. Christ on Calvary!

    Jehovah-Rapha means, "I am the Lord _____ _____."

5. What difference is this going to make in your life?

JEHOVAH Â€"NISSI: THE LORD OUR BANNER
EXODUS 17:8-15

1. Read the text carefully and answer the following questions.

    a. What were the circumstances involved in the revealing of this name to Israel?

    b. The Amalekites were a perpetual sore in the side of Israel. In this story, what parallel can you draw to contemporary Christian life concerning these people? To what in the Christian life can they be compared?

    c. To consider this question further, see Galatians 5:17. What do we war against continually according to this passage? See also Romans 7:21-24. What warfare is described in this passage

2. What led to victory for Israel over the Amalekites? Exodus 17:11-13

    See also Ephesians 6:18 and 1 Thessalonians 5:17. What do these verses add to your thinking?

    The victory of Israel obviously depended upon Moses continually standing before God and not being weary in his praying. What in the story suggested that prayer was involved? vs. 11-12

    What other strategies do you have in not giving way to the carnal nature in your life?

3. The Revelation of the Name Jehovah-Nissi; The Lord Our Banner, Exodus 17:15-16. This name has to do with warfare. In this instance, the warfare involved God's very own. Our Father is willing to wage warfare on our behalf. One area of great battle has to do with our carnal nature. List areas involving your carnal nature that are the most difficult for you to deal with.

    a.

    b.

    c.

The Lord Our Banner desires to give us victory. Read Romans 8 and learn of the victory that is ours over our carnal nature.

Life Application

Read through your journal and review your experiences. See how Jehovah has met your needs and how He lives up to all of your expectations.

Hope

*"The worst thing you can do in this economy is get a second job.
The best thing you can do is start a home based business."*
~ Dave Ramsey

I totally agree. The amount of time, energy, and money spent looking for a job and going to that job can be astronomical. God forbid you need a babysitter; you will immediately spend 60 percent of the pay from your second job. For these reasons and more, one of the best things you can do in life is figure out how to monetize your passion!

First, you have to determine what you are truly good at. What gift do you have that no one else has or that no one can do better? Put a name to it, create goals for yourself to put it into action, and *voila!* You are ready to start earning your true worth. Be aware, however, that there are steps that must be taken, for it is not a simple, linear path from Point A to Point Z.

There are no gifts too big or too small. As you can see from my co-authors' stories, everyone possesses their own, unique gift—and that includes you! It may be something as seemingly small as an advice column or as seemingly large as a construction company. You know yourself best, so it's your call. Whatever it is, just be sure that you're good at it, and be prepared to become a world-renowned expert.

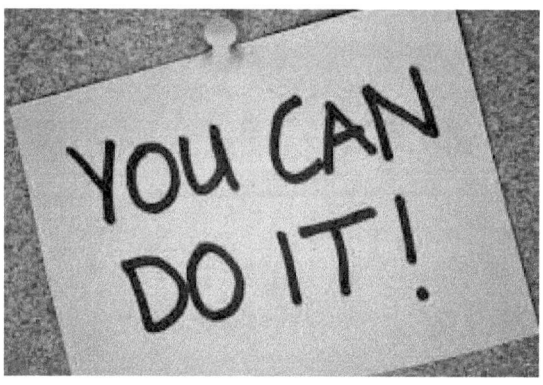

So now what? What do you do, and how do you do it right? In the stories you've read, we have given you tips and ideas to be the best of the best while avoiding pitfalls that can destroy all you've worked for. Take these lessons to heart.

First and foremost, though, you have to have a why. Why do you do what you do? Your why must be so powerful that you would cry if you could not fulfill this destiny. For some people, a why might have something to do with a family member, a promise, a pet, a friend, or just being tired of being tired. Below are questions for you to answer, and they will help reveal your potential business to you.

The next step is to find a trustworthy coach and mentor, and then you can start turning your dream into a business reality!

What do you love doing? _____

_____

_____

_____

Planning is everything. Do you have a clearly laid-out plan, such as a business and financial plan? _____

_____

_____

_____

Is there someone you can learn from? Do you know someone who's already successful at the business you want to undertake? _____

_____

_____

_____

What do you want in life? _____

_____

_____

_____

Do you know an expert marketer? If so, who? _____

_____

_____

_____

What is your idea of branding? _____

_____

_____

_____

What name will you register for your domain name? _____

_____

_____

_____

List two other names as backups. _____

_____

_____

_____

What is your vision for your website? _____

_____

_____

_____

Who comprises your market? _____

_____

_____

_____

Is that market saturated? _ _____

_____

_____

_____

Are you ready and willing to fail your way to success? _____

_____

_____

_____

Who are your biggest supporters and why? _____

_____

_____

_____

What is your why? Is it enough to make you cry if it isn't fulfilled?

_____

_____

_____

What is or has been stopping you? Can you overcome that obstacle? _____

_____

_____

_____

Believe in yourself and your abilities! Think about all the things you want to accomplish and those people you really want to spend time with. Congratulations! You just lost your J.O.B., so you now have time to spend with your family, friends, loved ones, and, most of all, yourself!

You owe it to yourself to succeed. Small businesses really do make the world go round, and they are the epitome of the American dream, so let's go for a ride!

YOUR LAUNCH: MAKE IT LARGER THAN LIFE

*I*t is time for you to use what you have learned from this book and make it happen for yourself! You have the tools. Now all you need is the faith to go through with it. Invite ten of your closest friends to help you with a virtual business launch and cut the ribbon before thousands of people, or flood the community with your business card and flyers.

A lot of people like hosting Twitter parties and hashtagging the event so it will trend. Make social media your friend. Also consider getting a free conference line to host calls in preparation for the event. One very smart investment is Instant Broadcast Pro (contact me at info@ awakethechampioninyoul.org to learn more about this awesome Peak Performers Institutes proprietary tool that will make your hangouts and videos personalized and stellar!) Whichever you choose, make it larger than life. A closed mouth is a closed business, and you don't want that.

After you master your techniques and become successful at what you do, you can now look in the mirror and say, "Congratulations! You just lost your J.O.B! Now who's the boss? I am!"

Here are the top ten MLM and small business ideas for you to consider, in the event that you want to own your time but aren't sure where to begin. Often, we just need a boost, a little push. Research these ideas for yourself and see if any of them may be your gateway to freedom. I strongly encourage you to take a peek at these companies by visiting their websites, and I look forward to hearing about your success!

10. Foreclosure Cleaners.

The bank has a huge job on their hands as it is, and they truly do not have the time to clean out a home that was just foreclosed on. This is where you come in! All you need is a business license, liability insurance, and an EIN/TIN number to start! Once you get those items (check your state to ensure that you are not in need of other credentials), it is time to broadcast your business. Send flyers to banks, sheriff's departments, and, of course, the paper. Make your name, website, and business card catchy, and you are on your way.

9. Mobile App Consultant.

In today's mobile-based, Wi-Fi-dependent times, if you are not using an automated system like the Penny Marketing System, you are in the dark. Consulting companies or individuals about the importance of mobile marketing is a huge breakthrough. Once you learn the industry, you can make changes in record time. Everyone checks their phones more often than email, so you will always be in demand!

8. Editor.

If you love to read and embrace getting first dibs on literary works, this is for you! First, you must make sure you passed English 101 for this job, as spelling, punctuation, and grammar knowledge will make or break your success. More and more experts that are creating their business cards through books, and you can get your name out there by editing a few for a discounted price and encourage testimonials.

7. Traveling Spa.

Yes, people are seeking downtime to ease their minds and help them wind down after stressful activities. Lisa Holland-Morgan is a specialist in this field, based in Philadelphia. She will show you how to capitalize on your business by attending trainings, workshops, conferences, and events that will help you teach and reach more. If you offer your services on the road, you can reach more clientele and broaden your brand. Her main focus is the customer and maintaining integrity. Her clients seek massages, manicures, pedicures, and hair styling. As long as you are certified and/or licensed in these areas, you may be on to a lucrative career, on your terms. There are many certification schools you can attend full or part time, and you should learn all you can to pass the exam.

6. Real Estate.

Yes, the market is screaming for those who are ready to sell short-sale, foreclosures, auctioned, and traditional houses. Charna Parler is a premium real estate agent for the Delaware/Pennsylvania area, and Tiana Von Johnson continues to dominate the luxury real estate industry. You can capitalize on this industry as well. Yes, you! With the MIA program, you can invest in a system that will get you started with a property (or more, depending on your investment) and allow you to keep buying and selling, earning money in the process. Email me today at Info @Awakethechampioninyou.org for more information.

5. Mary Kay.

This is one of the longest-standing beauty and skincare systems of modern times. Mary Kay Ash knew exactly what she was doing and was a brilliant businesswoman ahead of her time. It is very important to look and feel your best, especially as an entrepreneur. The company offers products that will help your skin look younger and fresher, as well as many other products that you can enjoy. Go to <u>www.MaryKay.com/RevReginaGray</u> to see what they have to offer.

4. Travel Agent Partner.

Paycations is a MLM company that provides you with all the amenities of an agent and a support team. As an agent, you will receive a multitude of training lessons, free trips, and an opportunity to earn six figures within the first year of business! How? They offer more than twenty-five ways to get paid, including high-commission payouts. Paycation Travel is the next best thing to owning your own agency. For more information or to join, go to, <u>http://aplus.paycation.com/index.asp?CO_LA=</u>

3. Social Media Expert.

Companies are using social media more and more these days, but they are not all familiar with the proper use of these important media tools, nor do all of them have the time to invest to learn it. That is where you come in. Offer stellar services with a guarantee that you'll put their company out there for everyone to see. If you want to take it to the next level, offer your customers Instant Broadcast Pro to maximize their social media experiences, providing a solution to their low visibility. Contact info@awakethechampioninyou.org for more information about Peak Performers Institute products and services.

2. Ardyss International.

This is a debt-free health and wellness company that gives you a chance to change your health and wealth all in one! Just ask someone if they'd like to drop two or three sizes, with no surgery and no pills, and you're almost guaranteed to get their attention in less than ten minutes. Ardyss specializes in a multitude of products; their hottest one currently is the corset, because people are training and getting "waisted." The signature Ardyss product is Body Magic and Levive. If you are into healthy living and weight loss, this is the business for you. Ardyss offers a chance for you to own a micro-franchise and earn big bucks while you are at it! For more information or to sign up, go to www.1derfulyou.com

1. Business Developer.

Yes, helping people live their dreams is the number-one small business. To be successful at this, you must like people and be prepared to dedicate your time to your clients, individually and collectively. You will be responsible for branding their business and sharing Business 101 information. You may create or design business cards or websites or coach your clients in thirty-second elevator pitches and presentations. This is a great opportunity for those who have strong marketing, economics, and speaking skills. Reach out to any of these great authors to find out how to be groomed for this awesome career.

ABOUT THE AUTHORS

*W*e are so excited that you are prepared to give your boss "the reverse pink slip," as Ruben West would say! Now, allow me to introduce you to all the dynamic authors who have contributed to this book.

Dr. Renee Sunday

Renee Sunday, MD is the founder and CEO of Sunday Publishing Company, LLC and RS Commerce, PC. She has practiced anesthesia for over thirteen years. Her mission is to encourage and empower others to enjoy life and obtain their dreams. Furthermore, she enjoys being an instrument in God's plan, rendering services to others and showing compassion, love, and a standard of care. She hopes to empower others to propel their message to the world.

Renee is a radio and television personality, host of *Good Deeds* radio and TV show and co-host of *Living Day by Day* on television. She is also a grief/loss specialist, group counselor, motivational/inspirational coach, passion/purpose guru, author, publisher, healthy coffee distribution owner, and an anesthesiologist.

Renee's passion is to be a catalyst to stimulate others forward, toward their destiny. For fourteen years, she thought her true purpose was to provide anesthesia services, until she went from six figures to zero in twenty-four hours. When one door closed, several new doors opened, and they continue to do so on a daily basis.

Everyone has purpose, a calling, a reason to be on Earth. A lot of people ask, "Why was I created?" They want to know their grand purpose in life. The truth of the matter is that many people are not called to one area or one thing; there are many things we enjoy in life. Can you say you are enjoying life? If you are frustrated with your job, career, or where you are right now, get purpose now with Dr. Renee Sunday. Encourage, empower, and educate others to propel their passions to purpose. One step will lead to an abundant supply of opportunities, obtaining dreams, and achieving a purposefully driven life.

Nisha Ray

As a single mother of three, Nisha is no stranger to life's challenges and truly speaks from experience. She offers strategies and tools individuals can use in the real world to maneuver through life transitions and conquer obstacles. Nisha equips her clients and other individuals to be more powerful, more effective leaders, both in their own lives and for others.

As with anything she touches, Nisha Ray brings her high energy, sharpened instincts, and sense of humor to challenging situations to order to inspire change, challenge herself, and gain new perspective. She understands that true change cannot happen without God as the foundation.

Nisha is a certified Christian life coach, certified life coach trainer, and certified anger resolution therapist, as well as a strategic interventionist student and evangelist.

Arlene Spann

Arlene Griggs Spann, a native of North Carolina, now resides in Maryland. She is a wife, mother, grandmother, author, teacher, and speaker, married to businessman Jerome Spann. She is the founder of Arlene Spann S.W.E.A.T.S., a business she created from her struggle of being unhealthy and overweight, after she successfully lost over fifty pounds. She uses this success as an example of how an obstacle can be turned into an opportunity to inspire and empower others to take control of every aspect of their lives so they succeed and reach their goals and God-given purpose.

Her educational successes include a "How to Start and Succeed in Your Own Business" certificate from Evangel Cathedral, with Bob Yates and Fred Foster. Her passion to see others triumph led her to become certified as a life, leadership, and weight loss coach via New Creation Coaching Academy in Maryland. As a woman of God, she earned a discipleship degree from Jericho Christian College.

She gives back to the community as facilitator of a free weight loss course through her local church. Arlene has been a guest on *Extreme Health*, a radio show hosted by Fred Foster. She has spoken on Blogtalk radio and appeared on Livestream. She is a member of the various organizations, including the National Association of Professional Women. Contact Arlene for speaking events, interviews, or media appearances at: ArleneSWEATS@gmail.com

240-354-9174 Toll free/fax 866-432-6896.

website www.ArleneSpannSWEATS.com

facebook:ArleneSpannSWEATS • twitter.com/arlenesweats

Jae Mello Spence

Jae Spence is a seasoned singer and theater actress who now uses her talents to help others as a vocal coach. She is a single mother of five, with children ranging from six to twenty-seven, the grandmother of one grandson, an entrepreneur, and author with two soon-to-be-released books to her credit, *Destiny* and *My Story but Not My Song*, in which she shares the story of her life as a pastor's wife, abused by her husband. She is passionate about helping others and dedicated to helping them bring their best voice forward.

Jae has been singing as ministry for years and was led one day to help others realize the power of song, emoting, and movement. In 2007, she started Melodious Vocals, "where we take your voice to the next level." At the time, she was working a J.O.B., until she was forced from the nest. Jae had been in the workforce for many years and finally flew out of that nest of safety, into her purpose, after feeling restless and uninspired while working for someone else.

She is currently working her dream by helping others see theirs. Jae inspires her clients to find their own voice. "Music can do wonders for the soul, and creating your song, using your voice and body, is known to be therapeutic," she says. She plans to one day open a Christian performing arts center and bring healing to the mind and body through song, dance and ministry. Jae has enrolled to pursue her master's in organizational management and therapy at LaSalle University this fall.

She says, "I realize through working with multiple people on various levels just how much expression can uplift the spirit. My focus has become to do more than just learn to sing, but to express, find your inner voice by writing and reciting, emoting, and feeling what you deliver! If you believe it, others will too." Jae also focuses on bringing out the confidence in each individual: "Singing and letting go…can be hard, but once you do, your life will be changed. 'Be inspired while inspiring' is my motto. Just think of how much one can accomplish if they are allowed to express, and what better way than in song, in poetry, in movement, and using your voice?" Jae served on the NK Arts Council, has created and offered group programs for the town of North Kingstown for seniors, Sing Yourself Happy and other Take an Arts Break programs. Another program Jae created for the town was Slam, where teens are encouraged to write poetry and recite it. This brings singing arts to after-school programs and neighborhood organizations. With the help of the humanities director, she also started the West Bay YMCA very first musical theater program back in 2010.

Currently, Jae serves as the musical director for North Kingstown Drama, a group that focuses on creating fantastic, youth-centered plays to inspire and bring joy to those who come out to see them. She says, "We work with sometimes over eighty young people, teaching them drama, singing, and dancing. In the end, they showcase a wonderful play. I've been with the group for six years now, and six plays later, I still look forward to the wonderful talent of the local youth."

Jae also helps in diction and engaging the audience. Even if you are not interested in singing or writing, Jae can help those who fear public speaking. The breathing technique she uses for singing does wonders for speakers. "Confidence is key," she says, "and that is my focus—to build confidence." Jae has helped radio personalities gain their voice with better ways to engage and pull in the listener. "I will create a program based on your desires. Programs for groups, schools, organizations, and private students—anyone looking to take their voice to the next level." Jae motivates others with her positive approach to life. Jae is called "Smiley" by many because she has learned to be happy inside and smile on the outside to spread the joy. Jae has overcome many obstacles and says, "The joy of the Lord is absolutely my strength. I could do nothing without God!"

Jae is available for bringing joy to you by coaching, singing, and motivational speaking. You can reach Jae at 401-219-6800. Video chat lesson are available to those who don't live nearby.

www.jae.vocalcoach@gmail.com • www.jaesings.blogspot.com

Like us on Facebook >>>Melodious vocals

Ruben West

Born in Topeka, Kansas, Ruben M. West is known as The Vision Breakthrough Expert. He is currently a seventh-degree black belt and was inducted into the U.S. Martial Arts Hall of Fame as Instructor of the Year in 2005. He co-founded two martial arts schools, both of which are still in business after fifteen-plus years. Ruben is a decorated combat veteran who served in the U.S. Army as a staff sergeant in *Operation Desert Shield/Storm* with the 410 Evacuation Hospital. He is the founder of The Success Immune System, a certified professional success coach, a trainer, an entrepreneur, a published author, and dynamic speaker.

He teaches and trains students and clients all over the world to step into their vision and, as he puts it, "Live your best life." Ruben has mastered the ability to help individuals see a larger vision of themselves and has developed a masterful system that allows individuals to increase productivity, improve relationships, and spend time doing what matters most. More specifically, he helps individuals get clear about what they want, break through any limitations, challenges, and/or limiting beliefs that may be holding them back, and ultimately help them achieve their dreams. For more information: Rubenwest360.com

Get Social: Fb/RubenWestSpeaks

Email: info@rubenwest360.com

Shavon Goodwin

Shavon Goodwin a resourceful single mother of six. She was a teenage mother who refused to be a victim of the hand she was dealt, and she reinvented her life with a changed perception and a forceful tenacity. Shavon has now fully stepped into her purpose as a passionate motivational speaker and author. She is said to have a fashionable, intuitive, and creative approach as she uplifts and re-creates the drive in women all around the world.

She is a compassionate, transparent speaker who inspires women to play their hand in life and to remain activated to thrive throughout their journey, which leads them to true love of self and their divine purpose

Felicia G. Meadows

Ms. Felicia Meadows is a professional school counselor with Prince George's County Public Schools. She has worked in the field of education for more than fifteen years and has experience at each level, from elementary to high school. In addition to being a counselor, Ms. Meadows is also a youth coach. She uses her skills and experiences efficiently to empower students, parents, and other individuals to create fulfilling educational and life experiences, which embodies her motto, "Step up your life." As founder and CEO of Tomorrow's Future Coaching and Consulting, Ms. Meadows assists young people in finding their passion and purpose to create the life of their dreams.

Ms. Meadows earned her bachelor of science psychology degree and master of education in guidance and counseling from Bowie State University and studied with the Institute for Life Coach Training to become a life coach. She has taken coursework in urban education at Johns Hopkins University to enhance her skills in working with diverse populations. In 2011, she utilized her skills and knowledge to facilitate a workshop entitled "Bullying 2011: The Mean Girls Phenomenon" at the Swing Phi Swing Annual Girls' Conference. Ms. Meadows also served as a panelist at the Middle School Forum in 2012 at Highland Park Baptist Church for their College and Career Symposium.

During the 2012-13 school year, Ms. Meadows was a member of Congresswoman Donna Edwards's Education Committee and served as moderator for the congresswoman's 2012 Annual College Fair. She will to continue working with Congresswoman Edward's Education Committee for the 2013-14 school year. She was spotlighted in 2012 on the Careers in Psychology website for her interview about her role as a school counselor at careersinpsychology.org/interview/felicia-meadows. One of her biggest accomplishments will be as part of a collaboration as a contributing author in the *Head Lady in Charge #HLIC* book, for which she penned a chapter called "How To Be the Head Young Lady in Charge," which will be launched in Spring 2014.

Felicia G. Meadows, M. Ed

Counselor~Coach~Consultant

felicia.stepupyourlife@gmail.com

(301) 523-8734 (c)

Sharlene R Prince

Sharlene R. Prince is The Royalty Mindset Coach who focuses on developing the riches in you by empowering you with the tools and resources that will unveil your buried treasures as you grow into becoming the best you possible.

Sharlene R. Prince strives for excellence in her humanitarian efforts, working with women and children to help them rebuild their lives after enduring emotional and physical abuse. She has been working with nonprofits for over twenty years and has formed her own, The Women Rising Above Group/The Women Rising Above Enterprise, Inc., which helps women and children to receive the resources and tools necessary to begin the next chapter in their lives. She has implemented the Commitment to Change (CTC) Program, which provides the necessary steps in rising above your circumstances and rejuvenating your life.

Ms. Prince continues her efforts internationally and nationally through her Women Rising Above Tour, which shares and advocates the message for domestic harmony to eradicate domestic violence and brings awareness of the verbal and physical abuse endured by women and children. She has been called "Queen of Possibilities" because she strongly believes there is a solution to every problem. She works tirelessly to resolve these issues and seeks the options necessary for their advancement. Her motto is, "Each one reach one as we rise above."

Sharlene is also an author and a royalty mindset consultant. Her most recent book, *The Royalty Mindset*, shares strategies in getting your mind right as you rise above. The royalty mindset demonstrates the necessity of replacing negative thinking with positive as you aim high and place your focus on the important essentials in life. It allows us the opportunity to advance our thinking skills and restructure the paths we choose in life. It helps us to build confidence in ourselves.

Ms. Prince has earned her bachelor's degree from Columbia College and her master's in human resource development and administration from Barry University. Through her networking and bridge-building, Ms. Prince continues to empower, embrace, encourage, and enlighten others who want to rise to their full potential as they take hold of their life and aim for their rightful seat on the throne.

Mia Zachary

Ms. Zachary is a bestselling author of ten books to date, the trademarked inventor of Noodle Cubes™ idea dice—an innovative tool for sparking "creativity anywhere, every time"—and the developer of From Mind…to Manuscript!™—an interactive workshop that guides participants from a story idea to a first draft in just two days—as well as Entrepubbing™—the first system for entrepreneurs to write a business book in about forty-eight hours. Mia believes your success is in your story and that everyone is the creative type. She can be reached at 702-763-CRE8 and <u>mia@cre8ivity3.com</u>

Ebony Archer

As a singer, author, speaker, entrepreneur, and TV producer, Ebony Archer is a force to be reckoned with. At the early age of four, she started singing in her church, where her gift was discovered. In the year of 2000, at the age of 8, Ebony joined Walt Whitman and the Soul Children of Chicago. With that group, she sang in front of audiences of ranging numbers, and she has shared the stage with many famous names in the industry: Yolanda Adams, R. Kelly, Celine Dion, Nick Carter, and more. In the year of 2001, Ebony Archer was featured in R. Kelly's video, "The World's Greatest."

Now twenty-two, Ebony is the CEO of her own entertainment company, Inspired by Purpose. She is executive producer of *Youth Speak Out*, a TV and radio show, and she is author of an upcoming self-empowerment book, Gotta Believe in Me. Ebony has already started a buzz with her new single of the same title, an inspirational song that motivates others to believe in themselves. With this song, Ebony will release a national Gotta Believe in Me Movement, and a documentary will be released In 2015.

Barrett Matthews

Barrett Matthews moves people from employee to entrepreneur. He holds people accountable for reaching their goals and dreams and makes them successful in the world of entrepreneurship. This is why he formed E2E Systems: "Do you have that desire to be the boss? Do you have a dream of running your own show? Do your goals keep getting stifled by your J.O.B., causing you to watch others do what you should be doing? Now is the time to take action and move toward your dreams, take on your desires, and achieve your goals. At E2E Systems, we merge our action-driven coaching programs with the inspirational training mind of professional speaker, Barrett Matthews to move you from working for a living to living your dreams."

Dwijesh Ramnath

Dwijesh Ramnath was born in Johannesburg, South Africa. He is an entrepreneur, author, dancer, motivational speaker, and founder of the NPO Power of a Teen. Ever since a young age, Dwijesh had been fascinated with art, creativity, and business. He was extremely successful as a teen and has continued that success as a property businessman, a dancer, and a motivational speaker. He graduated high school and did not follow the normal method of studying. Instead, he went straight into following his dreams, ideals, and his ability to help others.

Having been put in the worst situation after high school graduation, Dwijesh realized he had reached a make-or-break point in his life. He learned firsthand about devastating and tough times, and everything came crashing down. He decided to venture into something with the little he had. Having succeeded in a business with no help and no knowledge, Dwijesh became a success as a teen; thereafter, he created a nonprofit organization, Power of a Teen, and he debuted a book with a title of the same name. Dwijesh started helping teens and young adults find their passion and purpose.

Having followed his passion for dancing, writing, business, and speaking, Dwijesh believes life should be spent doing what means the most to you rather than following that which makes an individual unhappy.

As a dancer, Dwijesh has succeeded well. He has done shows for the *So You Think You Can Dance* SA media launch, Virgin Active. and Reebok. He has authored two e-books, both available on Amazon. com: His debut book was a self-help/semi-autobiographical book titled *Power of a Teen*, and his other is *The Positive Vibration Through Words*. Both books have changed and touched the lives of individuals. To help others is what Dwijesh believes in, and through his story and success, he has inspired others and helped schools of children, as well as individuals, achieve their best and grow every day.

http://www.powerofateen.org/founders.html

Mitsie Robinson

Mitsie Robinson is from Bronx, New York, and is the youngest of eight. Today, she is the proud mother of two blessed young men, whom she considers her inspiration.

In 1988, after being accepted for admission by several different colleges, she chose to enroll at Delaware State College (now University), to pursue a major in nursing.

Education and helping others has been Mitsie's purpose, her motivation to continue her own journey to success. She followed her dream and vision to become her own boss, worked toward her goal of entrepreneurship by employing the 3 D's: determination, dedication, and devotion. She attributes her success to hard work and putting God first.

In 1990, she was certified as a member of the Honor Society, and in 1991, she was nominated to be included in *Who's Who among Students in American Universities & Colleges for Outstanding Achievement in Nursing*. In 2001, she attended Wesley College to earn her advanced degree in nursing. In 2002, she was on the honor roll and was inducted into the Sigma Theta Tau Nursing Honor Society. In 2003, Mitsie earned her master's degree as a clinical nurse specialist in health promotion and illness prevention in the community. This allowed her to practice as a consultant, clinical expert, educator, and researcher.

Mitsie is now an entrepreneur, living out her vision, passion, purpose, and dream to help others. When she first had a vision to create her consulting practice, From the Heart Consultants LLC, her goal was to enrich, empower, and inspire others. Coupling her consulting skills with twenty-two-plus years of nursing expertise, her company offers a plethora of services that will surely reach the masses.

From the Heart provides mental health services, substance abuse consulting, recovery consulting, peer support, crisis intervention, health and wellness promotion, individual consultation, and grief and loss support. The company is based on the premise that we should all have a caring heart and that we should assist others in reframing their lives and their choices for more positive outcomes. Call today, and your life will be enhanced!

As a co-author of *Congratulations! You Just Lost Your Job!* Mitsie happily shares the story of her own journey to success, a life story that will encourage you to stay focused and to never give up on you!

LaSean Rinique

LaSean Rinique Shelton is an acclaimed international public speaker, radio personality, media strategist, and soon-to-be-published author of two books. LaSean has become a sought-after speaker in the industry, and she is prepared to break barriers and create stepping stones for the masses.

She was born and raised in Jamaica, Queens, New York, the oldest of three children. She attended August Martin High School and juggled cheerleading, mixing and editing for the tech crew, and various community service activities. Known as a motivator, LaSean encouraged her peers and those around her to do better and strive for better. In 1990, she graduated from August Martin and broadened her education by attending Delaware State University (DSU). There, she was dedicated and participated in many activities. Her most acclaimed memories include choir, cheerleading, and being lead actress in Dr. Damus Kenyatta's play production troupe, which later became a traveling production troupe.

After graduation, LaSean became a professional actress and was cast in several off-Broadway and local plays, as well as *Law and Order, NY Undercover*, improv troupes, commercials, local cable shows and several movies. Though acting was quite enjoyable, she felt something missing from her life. After being knocked down by life's many blows, LaSean learned her true purpose in life: to motivate and encourage others to be their stellar best.

Her first opportunities to motivate started at treatment facilities, institutions, churches, and small businesses. She felt alive and a sense of purpose, showing people how to manifest their vision to reality. Twelve years later, she has increased her market and is now experienced with assisting teams, families, youth groups, agencies, celebrities, churches, and individuals with stellar ways to brand or re-brand their products or services, all while motivating them toward success. Her energy is positively contagious, after you book LaSean once, you'll want to refer her and book her again!

LaSean launched Awake the Champion in You with a vision to improve as many lives as she can, one person at a time. As a social media strategist, LaSean Rinique, has the market cornered and locked when it comes to exposure. She teaches agencies ways to improve exposure and maximize their vision. As a transformational coach, LaSean reaches deep within her clients to grasp their inner voice and vision. As the motivator's motivator, LaSean assists in keeping coaches, professional speakers, supervisors, business owners, and leaders fresh and relevant. She also privately and discreetly works with celebrated clients with imagery, refocusing and edifying their careers. In addition to this, LaSean heads various outreach movements, always keeping the least of these in mind.

LaSean has served as a contributing writer for several blogs, national and international online magazines. She has hosted and co-hosted over fifteen radio shows, both terrestrial and Internet, over five television talk shows, and has a long acting résumé including movies and network television shows. In addition, LaSean has served in multiple speaker associations and symposiums, teaching the benefits of monetizing your worth on the web, how to use the media industry while simultaneously crushing traditional outlets. She has traveled through the States, inspiring many, and her message has resonated on the airwaves, YouTube, and beyond. LaSean has earned many accolades; however, her most prized and celebrated of them all are her three children, Anthony-Marc, JiHaad-Harmeen, and Aliya-Bernice.

To book or contact LaSean call (302)729-2280 or email her at Info@awakethechampioninyou.org • www.AwakeTheChampioninYOU.org

Dr. Paulette Clark

Dr. Paulette Clark has a diverse background in technology, ranging from telecommunications to terrestrial and digital radio. Hailing from the entertainment industry, Paulette has over twenty years of experience in media, entertainment, broadcasting and public speaking. Dr. Clark continues to work directly in the telecommunications and media industry on several levels, including Enterliant Services Group, which houses a call center for college students and part-time parents.

Dr. Clark also works closely with her team members at Cullen's Corner: The Brownstone, and she offers speaking engagements and life coaching, helping others to live life to the fullest.

www.ingramcontent.com/pod-product-compliance
Lightning Source LLC
Chambersburg PA
CBHW051213170526
45166CB00005B/1877